# THE PASTOR'S GUIDEBOOK

## A MANUAL FOR WORSHIP

Marion D. Aldridge

**BROADMAN PRESS**
Nashville, Tennessee

Grateful acknowledgment is made for the use of the following:

Prayers, Wedding and Ordination Statements: From A MANUAL FOR WORSHIP AND SERVICE published by All-Canada Baptist Publications for the Baptist Federation of Canada, copyright 1976.

Prayers, Declarations of Pardon and Ordination, and Committal Service: Reprinted from OCCASIONAL SERVICES copyright 1982, by permission of Augsburg Publishing House.

"Order of Service for the Parental Dedication of Little Children," © 1969 by Judson Press, Valley Forge, Pa. Used by permission of Judson Press.

Prayer: Temp Sparkman, *Writing Your Own Worship Materials*, © by Judson Press, Valley Forge, Pa. Used by permission of Judson Press.

Prayers, Excerpt on the Ring Ceremony, and Committal Service: From THE BOOK OF WORSHIP. Copyright © 1964, 1965 by The Board of Publication of the Methodist Church, Inc. Used by Permission.

Prayers and Declaration of Pardon: Reprinted from THE WORSHIPBOOK—SERVICES. Copyright © MCMLXX The Westminster Press. Reprinted and used by permission.

Prayer and Wedding Vows: J. R. Hobbs, *The Pastor's Manual*, © 1934, Broadman Press, Nashville, Tennessee. Used by permission of Broadman Press.

Parent-Child Dedication Service: Robert W. Bailey, *New Ways in Christian Worship*, © 1981, Broadman Press, Nashville, Tennessee. Used by permission of Broadman Press.

Prayer: Franklin M. Segler, *The Broadman Minister's Manual*, © 1969, Broadman Press, Nashville, Tennessee. Used by permission of Broadman Press.

Prayers: From MINISTER'S SERVICE MANUAL by Samuel Ward Hutton. Copyright 1958 by Baker Book House and used by permission.

Unless marked otherwise, Scripture passages are quoted from the Revised Standard Version of the Bible, copyrighted 1946, 1952, © 1971, 1973.

Scriptures marked KJV are from the King James Version of the Bible.

*To*

*Sally*

*Jenna*

*Julie*

*Mother, and Dad*

# Contents

Preface

# Preface

Monday, June 1, was my first day at work. I was a brand-new associate pastor at the First Baptist Church of Columbia, South Carolina. The secretary teased me that before the morning was over somebody would probably come across the street from the courthouse wanting to get married. Big joke! You can guess the rest. When the couple walked into my office at about 11:30 (beating noon by a full thirty minutes), I had no earthly idea what I was supposed to do to get them married. I would have given my first week's pay for some help!

I also remember my first funeral. Confidently prepared, I was seated by the casket in the funeral home. Suddenly my ignorance overwhelmed me. Did I walk out beside the casket, with the family, with the undertaker, or by myself? Help!

Other nagging questions came with other worship experiences. Why do we always baptize a person backwards? Forward looks so much easier. Why do we always go through a rather tedious ritual in removing a tablecloth from the *top* of the Lord's Supper elements? Would it be an ecclesiastical mistake to omit that step?

I needed answers. So I envisioned the kind of worship manual that would help me. Instead of including only poems, Scripture, vows, and prayers, this worship manual would also include brief biblical, theological, historical, and practical reasons for our various worship activities. Though traditional evangelical worship options would be retained, new possibilities would be explored. Above all, this worship manual would be a workbook for ministers.

*The Pastor's Guidebook: A Manual for Worship* is my dream come true. May every pastor profit from it. But, most especially, may every young pastor find the help (!) needed to begin a quality ministry.

MARION ALDRIDGE
Batesburg, SC

# 1
# The Lord's Day Worship Service

Without being told, you know how to worship. You responded to someone's worship leadership. Now you have followed God's call into the Christian ministry. You want to preach or teach or sing, and you want to lead a church in worship.

As ministers, however, we find ourselves in a predicament. At least I did. We give lip service to our spiritual forefathers and say that whatever we do must be based on solid biblical principles. Then we go to our first pastorate and worship using their traditions without a thought to biblical principles.

I quote one of my laymen who, I am sure, speaks for multitudes: "We sing a few hymns, take up an offering, hear a good sermon, and go home. What is wrong with that?"

As pastors, we need to be able to answer his question. We need to know both how to worship and *why* we worship the way we do. If God does have a preference, we need to worship *God's way*.

For the young minister, the "how" can be difficult enough. Don't we all remember the first time that we preached a sermon thinking that it would last for half an hour? But we discovered that we were through in six and a half minutes? You had seen your pastor make announcements and welcome the visitors, and you thought that such a simple exercise would come to you naturally, but your mind went completely, totally, and irreversibly blank when you tried it for the first time. Thank God for those patient congregations of all young ministers!

If figuring out "how" did not cause enough problems, there was always a "why" waiting in the wings. Why do many ministers "invoke" God's presence when God has already promised to be wherever two or three are gathered in his name? Why do we preach (offer salvation) week after week to those who are already Christians?

As a young pastor, I found some resources for the "how" of worship events. Finding out "why" was more difficult.

On any given Sunday morning in churches which do not have a prescribed denominational ritual, you will find almost as many forms of worship as you find churches. Just check the bulletins of several nearby churches. Neither music, nor Scripture, nor prayers, nor anything else is necessarily set. Some of these churches have litanies, confessions, and/or sermons based upon a lectionary. Others have no printed order of worship and are led spontaneously by the pastor and any number of other church members who feel "led by God."

Even so, some churches with seemingly less-structured Lord's Day worship services are the most rigid and inflexible in their liturgy.[1] People anticipate unwritten and even unspoken cues. A pastor friend of mine was chided recently by a member of his congregation who was concerned that he had dispensed with the "invitation hymn" during one of their Sunday evening services which had run overtime. This meeting, which seemed to be unstructured and informal, was more structured than the pastor had thought.[2]

The question for the pastor is not only "Which action is right?" (the question of "how"), but also "Why is a particular action right?"

*For the pastor who believes the Bible to be the inspired and authoritative Word of God, Scripture is the beginning place for any theological reflection on worship.* Historical considerations will also be significant because pastors must minister in the language and culture in which their people are immersed.

Unfortunately, the Bible has only scattered insights about worship. We have no clear and unambiguous description of a New Testament worship service. Nowhere are we told that you preach after the offering and the choir anthem. Nor are we helped a great deal by the Old Testament worship patterns. The sacrificial system and the law of the Mosaic covenant have been superseded by the unique sacrifice and grace of the Lord Jesus Christ.

Here are many helpful passages:

*Isaiah 6*—This is the "classic" passage around which many worship theories are built. The one holy God was praised. Isaiah confessed his mortality and sinfulness. God took away his guilt. Isaiah responded by saying, "Here am I! Send me." The emphasis is on God's holiness and grace and on Isaiah's response of submission.

*Joshua 24*—Joshua gathered the tribes of Israel and "they presented themselves before God" (v. 1). Joshua spoke for the Lord and told the people what God demanded, and the people responded by saying, "We also will serve the Lord" (v. 18). This worship experience stresses the covenant relationship between God and his people.

*Leviticus 16*—This is the priestly ritual for the Day of Atonement, emphasizing God's presence in the midst of his people and God's actions on their behalf.

*Psalms 15; 24; 77; 84; 100; 150*—The emphases in these Psalms are: (1) the Object of worship (God, who alone is worthy of worship); (2) the place of worship (the Temple in Jerusalem); (3) the character of worship (corporate thanksgiving or repentance); and (4) the character of the worshiper (righteous).

*Luke 4:16-21*—This account of Jesus in his hometown synagogue is the bridge between the old cultic worship of Israel and the new Christian worship. Jesus used the building, the Scriptures, and the teaching method of the Jewish religion into which he was born. But he poured new wine, new meaning, into the old wineskin, the old form. The methods would not hold the message. The wineskins burst, and new styles of worship began.

*1 Corinthians 14*—The major New Testament document of worship follows the famous hymn on love which gives the chapter its perspective. Paul's admonition to the Corinthian church is the most thorough description of New Testament worship recorded. It introduces some different concepts into the worship experience: the revelation, the amen, and speaking in tongues. It offers practicality and clarity as legitimate biblical reasons for making decisions about worship activities. Paul said, "I would rather speak five words with my mind, in order to instruct others, than ten thousand words in a tongue" (v. 19). Such reasoning appeals to us, as immensely practical people.

*John 4:21-24*—The dialogue between Jesus and the Samaritan woman emphasizes that true worship is spiritual, and the location of worship is insignificant.

*1 Timothy 4:13-14*—In this letter to Timothy, the public reading of Scripture, preaching, and teaching is required.

*Colossians 3:16-17*—This Scripture shows acceptance of music in Christian worship and emphasizes praise and thanksgiving. (See also Ephesians 5:18-19.)

*Hebrews 10:19-25*—The writer urges the readers to meet together, to encourage one another, and to keep the grace of God central in their worship.

*Mark 12:41-44*—The story of the "widow's mite" illustrates sacrificial monetary offerings in the context of worship.

*Matthew 18:20*—The presence of the risen Lord is assured wherever two or three people gather in Christ's name.

*Romans 12:1*—Using Old Testament cultic words, this

verse culminates New Testament worship theology. Paul appeals for each person to be a "living sacrifice" before God.

## The Purposes of Worship

The reasons for worship are limited. In worship God reveals himself to men, women, and children; and these same people respond to the demands of their Lord. These two purposes (revelation and response) are almost universally accepted throughout Christendom.[3] A third purpose is more predominant among evangelical churches. That third reason for worship is witness. Non-Christians are encouraged to observe the process of God's revelation and mankind's response in a worship service and then are invited to become a part of Christ's people.

A worship service may be predominantly witness.[4] Many English Baptist churches have evangelistic worship services on Sunday nights, and attendance often doubles that of the Sunday morning worship period. American churches often have evangelistic services on weekday nights. These are traditionally called revival meetings; and their purpose, despite their name, is usually to convert the lost rather than to revive the Christian.

## The Elements of Worship

Given these purposes of worship (revelation, response, and witness), the elements of worship should accomplish one or more of these objectives.[5] Due to restricted goals, the elements of worship are confined to relatively few activities which are listed below.[6]

*Affirmation of Faith:* a creed, covenant, or statement incorporating a body of doctrine.

*Amen:* an assent to another person's words. "Alleluia" or similar words, even applause, may serve the same purpose.

*Anointing:*[7] a symbol of (or the initiatory act in) healing.

*Benediction:* literally, a good word, spoken on behalf of God to the congregation.

*Blessing:* a prayer of petition, requesting the gift of God's grace for a specific person or concern.

*Call to Hear:* an invitation to worshipers to listen to the revelation of God.

*Call to Prayer:* the introduction to a corporate response to God.

*Call to Worship:* the initial words of a liturgy, commending worship to all hearers.

*Charge:* a challenge (or call to commitment) to an individual or group to live, act, or respond to Christ in faith and obedience. May also be known as the invitation.

*Confession:* verbal expression of contrition for sins.

*Declaration:* any pronouncement by the worship leader as a spokesman for God and the church. The pronunciation may signify the validity of a marriage, an ordination, or God's pardon of sin when a person repents.

*Dedication of Congregation:* for any group enterprise, the setting apart of something (new building, new hymnals) or someone (children and parents, Sunday School teachers) for sacred use.

*Dedication of Self:* the public or private commitment of an individual to God in a reaction of self-surrender to the revelation of God.

*Doxology:* literally, a glory word; an expression of honor to God, most often to the Trinity.

*Fellowship:* all concerns of the church, which may be as diverse as the welcoming of guests, congregational voting, or the announcing of church activities.

*Holy Kiss:* a token of Christian affection. May also be expressed by "passing the peace," which involves congregational members physically touching one another with handshakes or hugs.

*Intercessory Prayer:* a prayer on behalf of persons or groups, often including petitions for the church and its leaders, civil authorities, the poor and oppressed, and for local congregational members.

*Invocation:* calling for the aid (not the presence) of God in worship.

*Laying on of Hands:* a ritual whereby a person or persons are commissioned for special tasks (the professional ministry, the diaconate, missionary service).

*Offering of Material Gifts:* the act of contributing tithes and offerings to the church.

*Offertory Sentence:* a statement, usually preceding the offering, which calls the church to give in a certain way: either sacrificially or cheerfully, for example.

*Praise:* the expression of admiration of and homage to God.

*Preaching:* a sermon which proclaims the message of salvation (the gospel), usually to non-Christians.

*Teaching:* a lesson of the Christian faith, usually directed toward those who are already Christians.

*Thanksgiving:* the expression of gratitude to God for his work and his person.

Just as the reasons for worship are limited, so are the elements of worship. They may be called by different names, but there are only so many things that a group of people can do when they meet together before God in worship.

## The Methods of Worship

The methods of worship are a different matter, however. The number of methods that can be employed is limited only by the imagination of the worship leaders. Each method will serve one of the elements of worship, which will in turn meet one of the purposes. The following list of worship methods is suggestive and is certainly not exhaustive:

Address (or homily)
Architecture
Baptism
Cantata
Chants
Children's Sermon
Choir Anthem
Collect
Congregational Hymn
Film
Foot Washing
Fresh Flowers
Instrumental Music
Litany
Lord's Supper
Poetry
Quartet
Recording
Responsive Reading
Scripture Reading
Silent Meditation
Solo
Spontaneous Speech
Stained-Glass Windows
Symbols
Testimony
"Unknown Tongue" with Interpretation

As you can see, the methods of worship can be unlimited in their variety. Two, ten, or one thousand people can be involved in an act, such as a responsive reading. It can be done standing or sitting. It can be done solemnly or joyfully, loudly or quietly, simply read or dramatically performed, lay led or pastor led. A prayer or an address can be prepared or extemporaneous. Practicality, tradition, and the personal preferences of the congregation and the pastor should be considered. No intrinsic theological merit would favor one method over others.[8]

Much of the confusion over worship would be reduced if pastors and members perceived that there is a progression from the purposes of worship to the elements of worship to the methods of worship. The purposes of worship tell you *why* to include something in liturgy. The elements of worship tell you *what* you can include. The methods of worship tell you *how* to include it. The chart below illustrates the concept:

### Examples of Worship Strategy

| Worship *Purpose* | Worship *Element* | Worship *Method* |
|---|---|---|
| Revelation | Benediction | Scripture, Quoted by Pastor |
| Response | Confession | Congregational Reading |
| Witness | Kerygma | Children's Choir |

The issues of "dignity" and "good taste" get a lot of attention from some writers and teachers. Some speak of "a spirit of worship" when they should have used the phrase "the spirit of dignity." The two are not the same. The teacher or author who equates dignity with a worshipful spirit assumes the cultural task of improving the "form" of many of his or her less-educated and/or less-refined students. As worthy as that goal may be, it is theologically suspect in a study of worship. A more acceptable effort for pastors who minister in churches where the worship services have been largely spontaneous would be to incorporate more prepared material into their services as a means of encouraging more disciplined thought and commitment. This would help to avoid the pitfall of repetitiveness and lack of depth, two frequent results of spontaneous worship.

"Form or freedom" (Don't say "structure versus Spirit," which is a more pejorative differentiation!) is the theological issue in this debate. Paul's warning that all things be done decently and in order is an instructive biblical mandate here, but it must be balanced with a theology of the freedom of the Spirit of God (see John 3:3). Those who tend to advocate total freedom in worship are apt to run afoul of Paul's instructions at this point. Those who are tenacious advocates of form run the risk that, in that liturgical setting, God's people will be unable to respond to him as they are spiritually challenged.

Cultural improvement is not the goal of worship. Instead, the aim should be to prepare a liturgy which will provide a worship experience for those people who will be in attendance. Remember that a worship experience will involve having a revelation about (or from!) God, responding to God as he has been revealed, and witnessing to the non-Christian regarding the lordship of Jesus Christ.

In one church, this may be done with a gospel quartet. In another, it might be done with a Gregorian chant. One church may respond to enthusiastic preaching. Another may react only to scholarly dissertations. The value of each is equal if they all accomplish their designated tasks.

Worship may speak to our intellect, our emotions, or to our physical senses. Any worship service which speaks to only one of these is potentially lacking. Variety within a given service, and variety over an extended period of time, helps to ensure that the liturgy speaks to the total person.

Another concern is the content or theme of a given worship service, or of a given element within a liturgy. An Easter worship service would be decidedly different from a worship emphasis planned for a national holiday. An evangelistic service would assume a different structure from a service designed for the growth of Christians. Some worship periods are (of necessity) miscellaneous in nature, including a variety of emphases. A liturgy should usually follow a logical sequence, but there is no single style that is adequate for all occasions. Habit can be a burden, but it can be less destructive than change for the sake of change. If your church has been singing "Blest Be the Tie" at the end of its Lord's Supper services (as mine has) for more than one hundred years, then you are well advised to leave it alone, all arguments that it is an inappropriate hymn for response to your well-prepared meditational thoughts not-withstanding. (I do not advocate harmony for harmony's sake. But in matters of tradition, "leave well-enough alone" when there exists no overriding theological or ethical reason to create discontent.)

## Planning a Lord's Day Worship Service

Normally a church should be called together as a corporate unit. Individual prayers and preparation need to yield to a group thinking, praying, feeling, acting, listening, and responding in unison as much as possible. You may begin with praise or contrition, both natural postures in the presence of Almighty God. Be careful not to structure a confession of the same sins week after week. Such repetition would make a mockery out of a (supposed) response of repentance.

At some point, various concerns of the church fellowship need to be considered. If they are not major, as a church vote on its officers might be, early in the worship service is a good time. Otherwise, the very beginning or the end of the service might be better. Other miscellaneous matters not in keeping with the liturgical theme (if there is one), may be incorporated early in the worship period before the service climaxes both musically and sermonically.[9]

An offertory sentence is not particularly common but can serve to introduce in an effective way the worship segment which surrounds the collection of tithes and offerings. Since the collection is usually considered one of those miscellaneous events, it is unfortunately tucked into the service following a hymn sometime before the sermon. A good case can be made for having the offering at the conclusion of the service, after the message, and letting this act symbolically stand for our offering ourselves to God.

The sermon can be *a* highlight of the worship experience. Whether instructive or evangelistic, the sermon presents a supreme chance to lift up Jesus Christ as Savior and Lord. It may pull together the various elements of the liturgy and call for a specific response. Having a call for commitment requires having an opportunity for response. There should be an occasion provided when those who wish to respond to God's demands may do so—either publicly or privately. A structured confession would be as valid here as it would be at the beginning of the worship period. A period of silent prayer with organ music in the background would allow an opportunity for persons to respond, as would a call to the front of the sanctuary to share the response with the pastor. Whatever the method, an opportunity for response needs to be provided.

Finally, the service of worship traditionally ends with a benediction, a good word from God. Before the people retire from worship, the benediction provides one final uplifting revelation from God.

Using this general framework, many options may be used, as long as they are theologically appropriate, intellectually and emotionally reasonable, and at least moderately workable.

The order of worship which many churches have printed is not usually intended to be a theological document, but it should be informative and instructive to the person in the pew, beyond simply being a schedule or program of events.

A typical Lord's Day order of worship might look something like this:

Prelude
Call to Worship
Hymn of Praise
Concerns of the Church
Children's Sermon
Doctrinal Hymn
Call to Prayer
Morning Prayer
Choir Anthem
Scripture
Message
Call to Commitment
Hymn of Dedication
Collection of Tithes and Offerings
Choral Doxology
Benediction
Choral Amen

An evangelistic service might be structured in the following manner:

Prelude
Call to Worship
Evangelistic Hymn
Welcome of Guests
Scripture Reading
Intercessory Prayer
Solo
Testimony
Evangelistic Hymn
Youth Choir Anthem
Gospel Sermon

Call to Commitment
Hymn of Invitation
Postlude

A liturgy for a teaching and training service might be arranged like this:

Prelude
Hymn of Fellowship
Concerns of the Church
Doctrinal Hymn
Affirmation of Faith (Responsive Reading)
The Lord's Prayer
Quartet
Scripture Reading
Prayer
Instructional Sermon
Charge
Hymn of Dedication
Offertory Sentence
Collection of Tithes and Offerings
Prayer of Dismissal

## Calls to Worship

*A call to worship is most effective when spoken from memory.*

I appeal to you therefore, brethren, by the mercies of God, to present your bodies as a living sacrifice, holy and acceptable to God, which is your spiritual worship. Do not be conformed to this world but be transformed by the renewal of your mind, that you may prove what is the will of God, what is good and acceptable and perfect. (Rom. 12:1-2)

Trust in the Lord with all thine heart; and lean not unto thine own understanding. In all thy ways acknowledge him, and he shall direct thy paths. (Prov. 3:5-6, KJV)

O Lord, be gracious to us; we wait for thee.
Be our arm every morning,
our salvation in the time of trouble.
(Isa. 33:2)

Come to me, all who labor and are heavy laden, and I will give you rest. Take my yoke upon you, and learn from me; for I am gentle and lowly in heart, and you will find rest for your souls. For my yoke is easy, and my burden is light. (Matt. 11:28-30)

How great are his signs,
how mighty his wonders!
His kingdom is an everlasting kingdom,
and his dominion is from generation to generation.
(Dan. 4:3)

Lift up your heads, O ye gates; and be ye lift up, ye everlasting doors; and the King of glory shall come in. (Ps. 24:7, KJV)

## Invocations

God of heaven and of earth, for your blessings of the past week, we give you our thanks. For our sins of the past week, we humbly repent. Our hearts are filled with praise for your grace. We are awed that the Creator of our world would join us, and be in our midst, continually revealing himself to us. It is because of your revelation in Jesus Christ that we gather on this Lord's Day. Sharpen our intellect, our emotions, and our spirits so that during this hour we can see you more clearly, feel you more deeply, and respond to you more fully. In the name and for the sake of your Son Jesus Christ, we gather in prayer and worship. Amen.

Our Father, may our hearts and minds be united in your Holy Spirit as we gather to worship. Help us to put aside the distractions of the week and meet you during this hour. In the name of your Son, our Lord, we pray. Amen.

Almighty God, who hast given us grace at this time with one accord to make our common supplications unto thee; and dost promise that when two or three are gathered together in thy Name thou wilt grant their requests; Fulfil now, O Lord, the desires and petitions of thy servants, as may be most expedient for them; granting us in this world knowledge of thy truth, and in the world to come life everlasting. Amen. (St. Chrysostom)

Remember, O Lord, Thy Church: deliver her from all evil, perfect her in Thy love, and from the four winds assemble her, the sanctified, in Thy kingdom which Thou hast prepared for her. For Thine is the power and glory for evermore. (From *The Didache*, chapter 10, verse 5, translated by James Kleist, © 1948, Paulist Press)

## Confessions of Sin

Have mercy on me, O God, according to thy
    steadfast love;

according to thy abundant mercy blot out my
transgressions.
Wash me thoroughly from my iniquity,
and cleanse me from my sin!

For I know my transgressions,
and my sin is ever before me.
Against thee, thee only, have I sinned,
and done that which is evil in thy sight,
so that thou art justified in thy sentence
and blameless in thy judgment.
Behold, I was brought forth in iniquity,
and in sin did my mother conceive me.

Behold, thou desirest truth in the inward being;
therefore teach me wisdom in my secret heart.
Purge me with hyssop, and I shall be clean;
wash me, and I shall be whiter than snow.
Fill me with joy and gladness;
let the bones which thou hast broken rejoice.
Hide thy face from my sins,
and blot out all my iniquities.

Create in me a clean heart, O God,
and put a new and right spirit within me.
Cast me not away from thy presence,
and take not thy holy Spirit from me.
Restore to me the joy of thy salvation,
and uphold me with a willing spirit.

Then I will teach transgressors thy ways,
and sinners will return to thee.
Deliver me from bloodguiltiness, O God,
thou God of my salvation,
and my tongue will sing aloud of thy deliverance.

O Lord, open thou my lips,
  and my mouth shall show forth thy praise.
For thou hast no delight in sacrifice;
  were I to give a burnt offering, thou would not be
    pleased.
The sacrifice acceptable to God is a broken spirit;
  a broken and contrite heart, O God, thou wilt not
    despise.
(Ps. 51:1-17)

Almighty God, unto whom all hearts are open, all
desires known, and from whom no secrets are hid:
Cleanse the thoughts of our hearts by the inspira-
tion of thy Holy Spirit, that we may perfectly love
thee, and worthily magnify thy holy Name; through
Jesus Christ, thy Son, our Lord. Amen. (From *Occasional Services*, 1982 Lutheran)

Almighty and most merciful Father; We have
erred, and strayed from thy ways like lost sheep. We
have followed too much the devices and desires of our
own hearts. We have offended against thy holy laws.
We have left undone those things which we ought to
have done; And we have done those things which we
ought not to have done; And there is no health in us.
But thou, O Lord, have mercy upon us, miserable
offenders. Spare thou those, O God, who confess
their faults. Restore thou those who are penitent;
According to thy promises declared unto mankind In
Christ Jesus our Lord. And grant, O most merciful
Father, for his sake; That we may hereafter live a
godly, righteous, and sober life, To the glory of thy
holy Name. Amen. (From *The Book of Common
Prayer*, 1790, Anglican)

## Declarations of Pardon

If we confess our sins, he is faithful and just, and will forgive our sins and cleanse us from all unrighteousness. (1 John 1:9)

In him we have redemption through his blood, the forgiveness of our trespasses, according to the riches of his grace which he lavished upon us. (Eph. 1:7)

Almighty God, our heavenly Father, who of his great mercy hath promised forgiveness of sins to all those who with hearty repentance and true faith turn unto him; Have mercy upon you; pardon and deliver you from all your sins; confirm and strengthen you in all goodness; and bring you to everlasting life; through Jesus Christ our Lord. Amen. (From *The Book of Common Prayer*, 1790, Anglican)

The Almighty and merciful God grant unto you, being penitent, pardon and remission of all your sins, time for amendment of life, and the grace and comfort of his Holy Spirit. Amen. (From *The Service Book and Hymnal*, 1962, Lutheran)

## Affirmation of Faith

I believe in God the Father Almighty, Maker of heaven and earth. And in Jesus Christ his only Son our Lord; who was conceived by the Holy Ghost, born of the Virgin Mary, suffered under Pontius Pilate, was crucified, dead, and buried: he descended into hell; the third day he arose again from the dead; he ascended into heaven, and sitteth on the right hand of God the Father Almighty; from thence he shall come to judge the quick and the dead.

I believe in the Holy Ghost; the holy catholic church; the communion of saints; the forgiveness of sins; the resurrection of the body; and the life everlasting. (Apostles' Creed)

I believe in one God: the Father Almighty, maker of heaven and earth, and of all things visible and invisible.

And in one Lord Jesus Christ, the only begotten Son of God: born of the Father before all worlds, God of God, Light of Light, very God of Very God, begotten, not made, being of one substance with the Father, through whom all things were made, who for us men and for our salvation came down from heaven, and was incarnate by the Holy Ghost of the Virgin Mary, and was made man, and was crucified also for us under Pontius Pilate; he suffered and was buried, and the third day he rose according to the Scriptures, and ascended into heaven, and sitteth on the right hand of the Father; and he shall come again with glory, to judge both the quick and dead; whose kingdom shall have no end.

And I believe in the Holy Ghost, the Lord, the giver of life, who proceedeth from the Father and the Son, who with the Father and the Son together is worshiped and glorified, who spake by the prophets. And I believe in one holy catholic and apostolic Church. I acknowledge one baptism for the remission of sins. And I look for the resurrection of the dead and the life of the world to come. (Nicene Creed)

Having accepted Jesus Christ as our Savior and

having been baptized in the name of the Father, Son and the Holy Spirit, we prayerfully make this covenant with one another and with our heavenly Father: To maintain a receptive will to the leading of the Holy Spirit; To faithfully attend the worship services of our church; To give myself to regular periods of prayer and Bible study; To devote my time, talents, and financial resources to the work of God in and through our church; To maintain doctrinal standards in keeping with the teaching of scripture; To consecrate my home to be used for God's purposes; To minister to the social needs of our community and world; To bear my witness to the good news of Jesus Christ in word and deed to the non-Christian world; To care for and admonish my brothers and sisters in Christ; To treat my body as the Temple of the Holy Spirit; To maintain a Christian life style and Christian standards in the midst of a secular society; To unite with a church of similar faith in the event of my departure from this congregation. (Covenant of First Baptist Church, Batesburg, SC)

## Doxologies

*Two popular doxologies are most familiar in their musical setting: "Glory Be to the Father," and "Praise God, from Whom All Blessings Flow." But doxologies can be scriptural or spontaneous and should be used frequently.*

To the King of ages, immortal, invisible, the only God, be honor and glory for ever and ever (1 Tim. 1:17).

Blessed be the Lord, the God of Israel,
    who alone does wondrous things.

Blessed be his glorious name for ever;
   may his glory fill the whole earth! Amen and
      Amen!
(Ps. 72:18-19)

To the only God, our Savior through Jesus Christ
our Lord, be glory, majesty, dominion, and authority,
before all time and now and forever. Amen. (Jude 25)

## Calls to Prayer

Let us pray.

Let us seek God, and he will be found.

Ask, and it will be given you; seek, and you will
find; knock, and it will be opened to you. For every
one who asks receives, and he who seeks finds, and
to him who knocks it will be opened. (Matt. 7:7-8)

If you abide in me, and my words abide in you, ask
whatever you will, and it shall be done for you. (John
15:7)

Again I say to you, if two of you agree on earth
about anything they ask, it will be done for them by
my Father in heaven. For where two or three are
gathered in my name, there am I in the midst of
them. (Matt. 18:19-20)

Hear my prayer, O God;
   give ear to the words of my mouth.
(Ps. 54:2)

## Prayer

*Prayers in worship may be spontaneous or pre-
pared. Pastors should be careful not to do all of the*

*public praying for their congregations but should
constantly involve laypersons.*

Our Father which art in heaven, Hallowed be thy
name. Thy kingdom come. Thy will be done in earth,
as it is in heaven. Give us this day our daily bread.
And forgive us our debts, as we forgive our debtors.
And lead us not into temptation, but deliver us from
evil: For thine is the kingdom, and the power, and
the glory, for ever. Amen. (Matt. 6:9-13, KJV)

Lord, make me an instrument of thy peace; where
there is hatred, let me sow love; where there is
injury, pardon; where there is doubt, faith; where
there is despair, hope; where there is darkness, light;
where there is sadness, joy. O Divine Master, grant
that I may not so much seek to be consoled as to
console, to be understood as to understand, to be
loved as to love, for it is in giving that we receive; it
is in pardoning that we are pardoned; it is in dying
that we are born to eternal life. (Francis of Assisi)

God, our Father, guide our thoughts so that they
turn to you. Lead our spirits so that they seek yours.
Convict our consciences so that we are receptive to
your leadership. Help us to put our prideful ways
behind us and to fix our attention on your will for
our lives.
Today, Lord, we need the rest that worship provides, so that we can gather ourselves under your
care and be refreshed from the toil of the week. We
also need the assurance, Father, that you will walk
with us through the coming week. Help us to see the
good of your creation and appreciate it. Help us also
to see our abuses of your earth and your people, and

help us to change our sinful ways. With you guiding us, we can be all we are meant to be. That is good news, and we proclaim, "Alleluia!"

We pray for those who lead us in our church and in our government. May you give them wisdom, discernment, and courage to make decisions which are morally right. We pray also for those who can only follow, because they have neither the stamina nor the skills to lead, for they are poor and oppressed. We pray that their hunger would be alleviated, and that they would have clothes and shelter for warmth, and that they could see some beauty in the world around them so that their imaginations would be stimulated and kept alive in the midst of a dreary existence.

Many in our midst are anxious or ill today, Lord, and need your care. Heal them physically and emotionally, and let their renewed lives be a witness to your majesty. Guide us all, our Father, in your Son's way, and for his sake. Amen.

O Lord, our heavenly Father, Almighty and everlasting God, who hast safely brought us to the beginning of this day; Defend us in the same with thy mighty power; and grant that this day we fall into no sin, neither run into any kind of danger; but that all our doings, being ordered by thy governance, may be righteous in thy sight; through Jesus Christ our Lord. Amen. (From *The Book of Common Prayer*, 1790, Anglican)

*Many hymns may be read by the pastor or the congregation as prayers, or, for an evangelistic worship service:*

Our loving Father, we thank you for giving us so much: jobs, homes, transportation, health, friends. We acknowledge that when our lives begin to lose the joy that we had as children, when the burdens of life begin to surround us and stifle us, that we need to turn to you, the Creator of life, to find the key to the mysteries of life. In your Son Jesus Christ you have revealed your way for us to have the best of your world. We are drawn to him because in Jesus we see you. We understand your freely-given love only when we see the crucified Christ. And we understand that you have the power to conquer death and give us life. Open our spiritual eyes, Lord, so that we may see and worship you, the only true God.

Convince us that we need to repent and give up our false gods, whatever they may be: our time-consuming habits, our material possessions, our unhealthy friendships. We need to trust in Jesus Christ as our Lord and Savior, and we pray that during this hour, we would each let him take complete control of our lives. Help us to serve him. We pray, expectantly, in his name. Amen.

*For a teaching or training worship period:*

Almighty God, Savior and Lord, make us receptive to the leadership of your Spirit. Help us to be sensitive to your thoughts. Help us to make your ways our ways. Guide us out of our complacency and create an excitement in us to be more like you. Aware of your grace, we seek your forgiveness. Keep us from committing the same sins, Lord, to which we have grown accustomed. Instead, help us to grow up as mature Christians, learning more about you daily, and committing more of ourselves to you as we move through this life. Father, we want you to be Lord of all of our lives. We want to be your servants. We want to be your friends. We want to be your children. With the assurance that you hear and answer our prayers through our Lord and Savior Jesus Christ, we pray. Amen.

## Calls to Hear

Let us hear the Word of God.

Thy word is a lamp to my feet
   and a light to my path.
(Ps. 119:105)

All scripture is inspired by God and profitable for teaching, for reproof, for correction, and for training in righteousness, that the man of God may be complete, equipped for every good work. (2 Tim. 3:16-17)

## Charges
## (The Invitation)

It is my prayer and the prayer of our congregation, that all persons in this assembly who have never trusted Jesus Christ to be Lord and Savior will, without any hesitation, abandon their own lives to his care. Trust in the Lord; he is sufficient for your needs.

If your life has been lacking in the love, the peace, and the hope that is the birthright of a Christian, then I challenge you to commit your life to Jesus Christ, and let him be your Savior and Lord.

Behold, I stand at the door and knock; if any one hears my voice and opens the door, I will come in to him and eat with him, and he with me. (Rev. 3:20)

If you confess with your lips that Jesus is Lord and believe in your heart that God raised him from the dead, you will be saved. (Rom. 10:9)

Hitherto you have asked nothing in my name; ask, and you will receive, that your joy may be full. (John 16:24)

*Both spontaneous calls to discipleship and charges incorporated into the body of the sermon can be effective.*

*Often, in evangelical churches, a hymn of dedication is sung at the conclusion of a sermon, during which individuals are given the opportunity to respond (either privately or publicly) to the charge that has been given.*

*An alternate or additional opportunity may be provided for congregational response by concluding the service with the offering.*

## Offertory Sentences

What shall I render to the Lord
    for all his bounty to me?
I will lift up the cup of salvation
    and call on the name of the Lord,
I will pay my vows to the Lord
    in the presence of all his people.
(Ps. 116:12-14)

Honor the Lord with your substance

and with the first fruits of all your produce.
(Prov. 3:9)

Every man shall give as he is able, according to
the blessing of the Lord your God which he has given
you. (Deut. 16:17)

Take heed, and beware of all covetousness; for a
man's life does not consist in the abundance of his
possessions. (Luke 12:15)

Each one must do as he has made up his mind, not
reluctantly or under compulsion, for God loves a
cheerful giver. And God is able to provide you with
every blessing in abundance, so that you may always
have enough of everything and may provide in
abundance for every good work. (2 Cor. 9:7-8)

## Benedictions

The grace of the Lord Jesus Christ and the love of
God and the fellowship of the Holy Spirit be with you
all. (2 Cor. 13:14)

Now I commend you to God and to the word of his
grace, which is able to build you up and to give the
inheritance among all those who are sanctified.
(Acts 20:32)

He who has clean hands and a pure heart,
    who does not lift up his soul to what is false,
    and does not swear deceitfully.
He will receive blessing from the Lord,
    and vindication from the God of his salvation.
(Ps. 24:4-5)

Peace be to the brethren, and love with faith, from God the Father and the Lord Jesus Christ. Grace be with all who love our Lord Jesus Christ with love undying. (Eph. 6:23-24)

## Notes

1. The word *liturgy* is biblical (from *leitourgia*, meaning "the work of the people). Some churches are erroneously called nonliturgical because they do not provide a set order of worship. By definition, any order of worship, fixed or free, is a liturgy.

2. Doing the theologically "right" thing in worship without the understanding (and possibly the permission) of your congregation may be the "wrong" thing to do pastorally. Most people respond to a mixture of reason and tender, loving care. If their opinions are treated as significant, then they will treat yours that way, too.

3. There are fancier ways of saying this: worship is a recapitulation of salvation history. When we worship, we experience anew the old story of God's grace and the salvation of persons. Israel repeatedly fell into sin because they forgot the Lord's works (Ps. 78:41-42). Their best worship consisted of remembering the wonders of God (Ps. 77:11-15).

4. Care should be taken not to let all services of a church be for the sole purpose of witness. Christians need to be confronted with the attributes and demands of God, and they need to have a chance to respond to him just as the non-Christian has. In such instances, if the non-Christian is present, he or she will overhear the gospel.

5. For example, an affirmation of faith may both reveal something about God and also provide a vehicle for the worshiper to respond to that revelation. On the other hand, the Amen would be exclusively a response. Almost any of the elements may at one time or another be a witness. I understand that Dwight L. Moody was converted from the influence of the last four words of a prayer, "for Christ's sake, Amen." If an act does not reveal to the worshipers an attribute of God, or provide the worshipers with an opportunity to respond to God, or serve as a witness to God, then

it probably should not be an element in a worship service.

6. A problem of terminology arises immediately. We have a multitude of slippery terms. What is a sermon? It can be either preaching or teaching. Some words have different meanings in different traditions, sometimes legitimately, sometimes otherwise. In some churches, the benediction is the name that is incorrectly given to the closing prayer. Many think that "Praise God from Whom All Blessings Flow" is *the* doxology when it is *a* doxology. Ministers need to teach their congregations proper terminology.

7. Frequency of use has not been a criterion for inclusion on this list. What is rare in one church may be a weekly practice in another. If your church seldom (or never!) uses a particular element of worship, you may consider some sort of trial period during which an opportunity is given to experience that element in a worship context. For example, I discovered that our church members responded positively to a corporate confession of faith.

8. Some people argue for repetition in worship: this allows the worshiper to become familiar with what normally occurs, and he or she can concentrate on worshiping rather than merely listening to the pastor worship. Others argue against repetition, fearing that worship may too easily become monotonous, boring, and futile.

9. The sermon is not the most important part of the worship period to many in attendance, although to many evangelical congregations, the primacy of preaching is an integral part of their worship theology. The gospel may be proclaimed in a multitude of ways besides the pastor's address. These methods might include testimony, Scripture reading, song, or litany.

# 2
# The Baptismal Service

Baptism is the initiation rite into the Christian church. That much is certain. Little else is. Christians manage to disagree on three aspects of the baptismal ceremony: the method, the subject, and the significance.

At least five major methods of baptism have been practiced at sundry points in Christian history. The most popular and theologically preferred method among contemporary evangelicals is single immersion. Single immersion involves the "burial" of the person being baptized completely under water (totally submerged). The symbolism is of the death of the old (pre-Christian) self, its burial, and the resurrection of the new person into a new life.[1] Usually a baptismal formula is spoken by the baptizer,[2] and a public confession on the part of the convert is often required.

The second method of baptism is similar to the first, but it involves a triple instead of a single immersion. The rationale behind this practice emphasizes the Trinity in the baptismal formula, "I baptize you in the name of the Father, and of the Son, and of the Holy Spirit." The convert is immersed after each name in the Trinity is mentioned, for a total of three immersions. This practice was most popular in early church history when controversy raged over the Trinitarian nature of God. Triple or triune immersion became an important test of orthodoxy.

Another method of baptism is dipping, which is a variation of total immersion. This would more often be practiced with children who could be held by the baptizer.

The candidate's left side would be dipped into the water, then the right side, and finally the face.

Pouring is a form of baptism that most vividly recalls the religious libations of the world into which Jesus was born. Their symbolism centered more around the idea of the washing off of the old sins than the complete burial of the old person.

The final method of baptism practiced within the church is known as sprinkling. I am impressed with the honesty of many theologians from denominations that sprinkle who candidly admit that the rich biblical imagery surrounding baptism must be left behind when one practices this method of baptism. Ecumenical dialogue has been mostly one-sided in this regard, with the nonimmersing traditions increasingly committing themselves to a more biblical awareness and practice (at least with adult converts).

Still, these five methods do not exhaust the possibilities, because of the almost limitless combinations of worship acts that have been associated with baptism. At some point in history, baptism has been practiced hand in hand or side by side with exorcisms, laying on of hands, anointings, and confessions of faith. Baptismal candidates have been required to face the East during the baptism, and they have been given milk and honey to drink and eat to signify their entrance into the Promised Land.

Along with the method of baptism, the subject or recipient of baptism has been a source of controversy. Who should be baptized? New Christians or the children of Christians? Believers or babies? Most evangelical denominations would insist that only believers should be baptized. This insistence usually eliminates the baptism of infants who are unable to make a decision of faith on their own.

The third area of baptismal theology which would affect our worship beliefs is the question of significance. What does baptism mean? Is it merely a symbol or is it a means of grace? Many Evangelicals prefer the word *ordinance* while other traditions use the word *sacrament*. By "ordinance," those who use the term refer to those symbolic acts instituted or ordained by the Lord Jesus, usually limited to two: baptism and the Lord's Supper. Some would include footwashing. Those who use the term *sacrament* generally make reference to a visible act which confers grace on the recipient.

I do not believe that any act in worship, including baptism, is automatically a vehicle for God's Spirit and power. God is far too interested in relationships to impose on us from above. If we just go through the motions, by saying the Lord's Prayer or by being baptized or by aimlessly participating in any other worship act, then we are unlikely to be recipients of God's grace—in spite of our activity!

This has a very important effect on why we baptize. We do not hurry a person into the baptismal waters because we think that he or she is unsaved until the act of baptism. A person's new birth begins at the time when he or she, in repentance, begins to trust God through Jesus Christ as Lord and Savior. A person is not regenerated in baptism. Through the act of baptism, however, God may speak to either the person being baptized or to a witness of the baptismal event in a mighty and miraculous way. At our church, we have seen people become Christians by responding to the witness of a Christian baptismal service. Conversely, I have baptized some people who, to my sorrow, disappeared from the life of the church immediately after their baptism.

I believe that sound theology places baptism, the Lord's Supper, and other acted signs in worship somewhere between being a "mere symbol" and being an "inevitable means of grace."

## Planning a Baptismal Service

Baptism should be removed from the Sunday night ghetto
to which it has been banished for so long in many churches.
It is entirely possible that some fairly faithful Sunday
morning worship attenders have not seen a baptismal
service in years. Baptism should also be given the opportunity to stand alone as the center of worship instead of being
tacked on at the beginning or end of a rather routine Lord's
Day worship. Enough hymns have been written and enough
Scripture exists concerning baptism to build a meaningful
and full worship period around this one important initiatory
event into the Christian family.

Baptismal services are excellent evangelical opportunities, and I like to present the simple, yet profound,
characteristics of the salvation act to the congregation
throughout the service. Therefore, Calls to Worship might
be John 3:16, Revelation 3:20, and similar Scripture.
Similarly, to close with Scripture such as Matthew 28:19-20,
Acts 1:8, and John 20:21 would be appropriate.

A baptismal service would be an excellent time for the
congregation to affirm their faith with a traditional creed.
Music and Scripture should point to the baptismal event. If
there is to be a sermon or spoken meditation, the nature of
the remarks would determine whether they should precede
or follow the actual baptism. In any case, the baptism
should be the climax of the worship period, with all the
other worship elements either building up to or resulting
from the baptismal act.

Several things occur as part of the baptism itself. Some
pastors like to quote New Testament Scripture from memory
while they are standing in the baptistry. When the choice is
appropriate, such as Acts 8:26-38, this can be quite meaningful. At verse 36, water may be cupped in the hand and/or
agitated by the pastor, emphasizing the material aspect of

the event without de-emphasizing the spiritual.

The name of the person being baptized should be mentioned, either in an introduction ("I present to you our first candidate for baptism this morning, Mrs. Jane Doe.") or as part of the baptismal formula ("I baptize you, Jane Doe . . . "). No ecclesiastical merit or demerit is involved in the use of either given names or nicknames. Personal preference may prevail.

A confession of faith by the new Christian can add a meaningful dimension to the baptismal service. Without this spoken involvement, the person being baptized is only a passive participant in one of the most important events in his or her life. I have found that even the most bashful person has appreciated this element of worship. A question or two may be asked the new Christian which he or she can answer in front of God's people.

The baptismal formula is a sentence or two spoken by the pastor during the act of baptism. I would normally appeal to the Trinity and describe the event taking place. However, no scriptural precedent exists for any particular words or phrases. Scripture (again, John 3:16 is a good example) may be quoted, or silence may prevail.

At the end of every baptismal service an opportunity should be given for those in the congregation to make or renew a commitment to the Lord Jesus Christ. Non-Christian family and friends will be present for this important occasion, and they may wish to respond to the nonverbal sermon that has been preached in the baptismal event.

A suggested order of worship might be:

Prelude
Call to Worship
Affirmation of Faith: Congregation
Doxology: Gloria Patri
Hymn of Praise
Collection of Tithes and Offerings

Morning Prayer
Evangelistic Hymn
Old Testament Scripture
Spoken Meditation
Choral Anthem
New Testament Scripture
Affirmation of Faith: Baptismal Candidate
Declaration of Baptism
Hymn of Commitment
Scriptural Charge
Postlude

## Calls to Worship

For God so loved the world that he gave his only Son, that whoever believes in him should not perish but have eternal life. (John 3:16)

If you confess with your lips that Jesus is Lord and believe in your heart that God raised him from the dead, you will be saved. For man believes with his heart and so is justified, and he confesses with his lips and so is saved. (Rom. 10:9-10)

He who believes and is baptized will be saved; but he who does not believe will be condemned. (Mark 16:16)

And Peter said to them, "Repent, and be baptized every one of you in the name of Jesus Christ for the forgiveness of your sins; and you shall receive the gift of the Holy Spirit." (Acts 2:38)

For by one Spirit we were all baptized into one body—Jews or Greeks, slaves or free—and all were made to drink of one Spirit. (1 Cor. 12:13)

For as many of you as were baptized into Christ have put on Christ. There is neither Jew nor Greek, there is neither slave nor free, there is neither male nor female; for you are all one in Christ Jesus. (Gal. 3:27-28)

## Affirmations of Faith for the Congregation

That we worship one God in Trinity, and Trinity in Unity; Neither confounding the Persons: nor dividing the substance. For there is one Person of the Father: another of the Son: and another of the Holy Ghost. But the Godhead of the Father, of the Son, and of the Holy Ghost, is all one: The Glory equal, the Majesty coeternal. Such as the Father is: such is the Son: and such is the Holy Ghost. The Father uncreated: the Son uncreated: and the Holy Ghost uncreated. The Father incomprehensible: the Son incomprehensible: and the Holy Ghost incomprehensible. The Father eternal: the Son eternal: and the Holy Ghost eternal. And yet they are not three eternals: but one eternal. As also there are not three uncreated: nor three incomprehensibles, but one uncreated: and one incomprehensible. So likewise the Father is Almighty: the Son Almighty: and the Holy Ghost Almighty. And yet they are not three Almighties: but one Almighty. So the Father is God: the Son is God: and the Holy Ghost is God. And yet they are not three Gods: but one God. (Excerpt adapted from the Athanasian Creed)

It is necessary to everlasting salvation: that he also believe rightly the Incarnation of our Lord Jesus Christ. For the right Faith is, that we believe and confess: that our Lord Jesus Christ, the Son of God, is God and Man; God, of the Substance of the

Father; begotten before the worlds; and Man, of the Substance of his Mother, born in the world. Perfect God: and perfect Man, of a reasonable soul and human flesh subsisting. Equal to the Father, as touching his Godhead: and inferior to the Father as touching his Manhood. Who although he be God and Man; yet he is not two, but one Christ. One; not by conversion of the Godhead into flesh: but by taking of the Manhood into God. One altogether; not by confusion of Substance: but by unity of Person. For as the reasonable soul and flesh is one man: so God and Man is one Christ. (Excerpt adapted from the Athanasian Creed)

## Baptismal Prayer

It is right for us to call you Father on this occasion when we witness visually the miracle of rebirth. We who have been your children joyously welcome new brothers and sisters into our Christian family.

Thank you, God, for caring for us in such an intense and obvious way. Thank you for the gift of salvation which you provide through your Son, Jesus Christ. Thank you for the gift of purpose and spiritual power which you provide through your Holy Spirit.

We confess that it is too easy to drift from one another. Help us, as we follow you and respond to you, to be an example to those (or the one) who will be baptized today, as we love (him/her/them) even as you have loved us. Help us to be sensitive to our responsibility to new Christians, sacrificing our own time and comforts in order to minister to their needs.

Never let us forget the significance of this moment in the life of the church. We are reminded of the Scripture that tells us of the joy in heaven when a sinner repents. Keep the eternal importance of this moment before us. We pray in Christ's name. Amen.

Creator God, the picture that you paint for us today is vivid. Just as your Son Jesus was buried in the grave and rose again victorious over death, even so today in baptism we see that victory repeated. Those who have been dead in sin and guilt will rise to walk in a new life.

Never let us become accustomed to this most significant event in the life of the church. Make it new and fresh and meaningful each time we witness it, for Jesus' sake. Amen.

Almighty and everlasting God, the aid of all who need, the helper of all who call upon thee for comfort, the life of all who believe, and the resurrection of the dead: We call upon thee for these (this) thy servant(s), that he/she, coming to thy holy Baptism, may receive remission of his/her sins and be filled with the Holy Spirit. Receive him/her, O Lord, as thou hast promised by thy well-beloved Son, and grant that he/she may be faithful to thee all the days of his/her life, and finally come to the eternal kingdom which thou hast promised; through Jesus Christ our Lord. Amen. (From *The Book of Worship*, 1964, Methodist)

*These statements of personal faith are usually spoken when both the candidate for baptism and the pastor are already in the baptismal water.*

## Affirmation of Faith for the Baptismal Candidate

PASTOR: _____, do you confess that Jesus Christ is Lord?

BAPTISMAL CANDIDATE: I do.

PASTOR: By your profession of faith in Jesus Christ, you, _____, are eligible to be baptized. Before Christ and these witnesses, do you confess your sins and do you acknowledge Jesus Christ to be your Savior and Lord?
BAPTISMAL CANDIDATE: I do.

*The candidate may be allowed to give his or her testimony, or the pastor may share it on behalf of the candidate.*

## Declarations of Baptism

I baptize you, _____, in the name of the Father, the Son, and the Holy Spirit. You are buried with Christ in death. You rise again to walk in a new life.

Upon the authority of Jesus Christ, the Head of the Church, and in obedience to the Great Commission, I baptize you, _____, in the name of the Father, and of the Son, and of the Holy Spirit.

In obedience to the command of our Lord Jesus Christ, and upon your confession of faith in him, I baptize you, _____, in the name of the Father, and of the Son, and of the Holy Spirit.

## Scriptural Charges

But you shall receive power when the Holy Spirit has come upon you; and you shall be my witnesses in Jerusalem and in all Judea and Samaria and to the end of the earth. (Acts 1:8)

Go therefore and make disciples of all nations,

baptizing them in the name of the Father and of the Son and of the Holy Spirit, teaching them to observe all that I have commanded you; and lo, I am with you always, to the close of the age. (Matt. 28:19-20)

Jesus said to them again, "Peace be with you. As the Father has sent me, even so I send you." (John 20:21)

And this is the testimony, that God gave us eternal life, and this life is in his Son. He who has the Son has life; he who has not the Son of God has not life. (1 John 5:11-12)

## Notes

1. Though the issue of "significance" will be considered later, it intrudes already. Suffice it to say that baptism is not a magic trick, and exact replication of details is not necessary. I have in mind the problem of an "incomplete" immersion, when the person being baptized ends up with a dry or unbaptized hand or lock of hair. In such a case, the baptism is not invalidated.

As a practical matter, the young worship leader would be well advised to "practice" baptism with a more experienced pastor who should be able to provide numerous helpful hints that will produce a smoother service.

Still, remember that beauty is not the goal of a baptismal service. As laudable as a picturesque service might be, there may be some splashing and coughing, and both the baptismal candidates and the baptizer should be aware that these do not make a less valid event.

2. An ordained minister is not necessary to conduct a baptismal service (or to lead in any other worship service) in any denomination which seriously believes in the priesthood of all believers. Anyone who is designated by the local church may perform these services.

# 3
# The Lord's Supper Service

The Lord's Supper is a worship service with rivaling emotions. I had hints of this early in my ministry, but I could never quite put my finger on the problem. My first real perception of a conflict between the two competing natures of the service came on a Maundy Thursday.

At our annual Maundy Thursday worship service, I had emphasized the somber dimensions of the Last Supper. With this supper we remembered the last days of Jesus. I reminded my church that "Sunday's coming!" but the mood for the evening was one of grief, sadness, and loss. The room was darkened, and the atmosphere was subdued. In my remarks, I questioned the wisdom and accuracy of our calling the Lord's Supper a celebration.

Immediately after the meal and the dismissal of the assembly, one of our church's teenagers challenged my statement about the Lord's Supper *not* being a celebration. He contended that it was. I knew the arguments, and they were good. The celebration of the Lord's Supper was a result of our remembering the grace of the Lord as exemplified by his atoning death on the cross. How could we help but rejoice at the goodness of God?! And of course, Sunday did come, and Jesus did conquer death, and a Christian's theology of the crucifixion cannot ignore the resurrection. So we celebrate! We are reminded of both the crucifixion and the resurrection of Jesus every time we participate in this meal of remembrance.[1]

My predominant memory of many Lord's Supper services

in my earliest childhood church was the careful way the pastor and the deacon chairman folded the cloth that was always on top of the trays that held the grape juice vials and the saltine crackers. The sacredness of that tablecloth always intrigued me more than the stingy portions of food that I was served.[2]

My error was typical. The outward acts and circumstances of the Lord's Supper worship service frequently overshadow the spiritual significance of the event. Questions abound, but so do answers. What some answers lack in theological perception, they more than compensate for in their dogmatic assurance.

## Planning a Lord's Supper Service

In a study of the liturgy of the Lord's Supper, the contemporary church would do well to return to basics. The words of the institution of the Last Supper are found in Mark 14:22-25. Though such a celebration may seem austere, it would never be inappropriate to restrict a communion service to these bare essentials: taking the bread as Jesus did, giving thanks, breaking the bread, and giving it to the disciples (and repeating the process for the cup).

From this base, many possible variations might emanate. Presuming that the standard Lord's Supper worship service is held *in* your church sanctuary *on* Sunday morning *with* wafers and grape juice served by the pastor, then a plethora of options are available to you simply by altering the place, the time, and the methods of the service. A study of the Bible will recommend many such changes, none of which are necessary, but each of which is instructive and/or inspiring in the proper context.

The Corinthian passage has challenged me to celebrate the *agape* or love feast in our fellowship hall. As part of a churchwide supper, we ended the regular meal by partaking of the Lord's Supper.

The Last Supper of our Lord has been commemorated by many churches on Maundy Thursday evening. A smaller attendance than the usual Sunday morning gathering allows for more intimate experiences—permitting, for example, the pastor to serve everyone individually if that is not customary. On one such occasion I served our church members three or four at a time as I seated them around the altar table as if they were at a restaurant.

Besides changes in place and time, Scripture suggests (either directly or indirectly) many alternate methods of celebrating Communion. John's Gospel tells of a foot washing on the night of the Last Supper (John 13:1-17). First Corinthians 10:1-4, using allegory, describes baptism and the Lord's Supper as consecutive acts and prompts the notion of including both, when possible, in the same worship period. Once, as a young pastor, totally by accident and ignorance, I served the cup first. Everyone was kind enough to forgive the oversight at the time, but that didn't keep me from hearing about it the next week. The mistake turned into a good opportunity to examine with the congregation Luke 22:14-20 (where the cup is served both before and after the bread) and to discuss some normally neglected aspects of the Last Supper.

One innovative pastor served cookies and Kool-Aid, emphasizing the commonness of the bread and wine in the day of Jesus.

Besides the simple amplification and alteration of the essential elements of the Lord's Supper, we would do well to let church history instruct us. Very early in Christian history, the Lord's Supper became one of the primary means of recalling salvation history. A prayer of thanksgiving for all of God's good works was an important part of some of the most ancient Lord's Supper services. Similar recitals had long been a part of the Jewish heritage (see 1 Samuel 12, Psalm 78, Isaiah 51, and Hebrews 11) and quickly became a part of the Christian tradition (see Acts 7, Acts 13, and 1 Corinthians 10 where the recitation is attached in meaning to the Lord's Supper). Since such a recapitulation of salvation history is both biblical and practical (in that it achieves the worship purpose of revealing God), a time of remembrance such as the Lord's Supper service would be ideal for its implementation. The element or method is incidental, with the historical information being incorporable into affirmations of faith, prayers of thanksgiving, didactic sermons or confessions, to name just a few options. The undiluted Scripture readings listed above might be used.

After references to ancient Judeo-Christian traditions, in a worship service, these beautiful and meaningful words from the Gloria Patri are generally appropriate: "As it was in the beginning, is now, and ever shall be, world without end. Amen."

Another ancient practice that has recently been restored in some churches is the "kiss of peace." Whether a kiss or a handshake or a kind word is the actual expression of this act of fellowship, it allows for the visible enactment of the demands of Jesus in Matthew 5:23-24 to make amends with your Christian brothers and sisters before approaching God's altar.

The hymn at the conclusion of the supper, recorded only by Matthew, has in recent years tended to be the fellowship hymn, "Blest Be the Tie." Though this is certainly an appropriate hymn, many twentieth century folks need to be reminded that Jesus and his disciples sang something different. In fact, scholars feel that something definitive can be stated about some of the hymnody/psalmody of the Last Supper. Psalms 113—118 were a typical part of Jewish festival seasons. The first two of these Psalms were sung before the Passover meal, and the last four of these "Hallelujah Psalms" were sung after the meal. Incorporating these into the Christian Communion service would be acknowledging their importance in our heritage.[3]

An order of worship for the Lord's Supper could be developed in the following way:

Invocation
Old Testament Scripture
Hymn
The Kiss or Handshake of Peace
New Testament Scripture
Affirmation of Faith
Gloria Patri
Confession of Sin
Sermon
Distribution of the Bread
First Prayer of Thanksgiving
Distribution of the Cup
Second Prayer of Thanksgiving
Choral Anthem
Hymn of Dismissal

## Calls to Worship

O Lord, be gracious to us; we wait for thee.
    Be our arm every morning,
    our salvation in the time of trouble.
(Isa. 33:2)


Lord, thou hast been our dwelling place
    in all generations.
Before the mountains were brought forth,
    or ever thou hadst formed the earth and the world,
    from everlasting to everlasting thou art God.
(Ps. 90:1-2)


And he said to all, "If any man would come after me, let him deny himself and take up his cross daily and follow me." (Luke 9:23)

And this is the testimony, that God gave us eternal life, and this life is in his Son. He who has the Son has life; he who has not the Son of God has not life. (1 John 5:11-12)

## Old Testament Scripture Readings

"Hear, O Israel: The Lord our God is one Lord; and you shall love the Lord your God with all your heart, and with all your soul, and with all your might. And these words which I command you this day shall be upon your heart; and you shall teach them diligently to your children, and shall talk of them when you sit in your house, and when you walk by the way, and when you lie down, and when you rise. And you shall bind them as a sign upon your hand, and they shall be as frontlets between your eyes. And you shall write them on the doorposts of your house and on your gates.

"And when the Lord your God brings you into the land which he swore to your fathers, to Abraham, to Isaac, and to Jacob, to give you, with great and goodly cities, which you did not build, and houses full of all good things, which you did not fill, and cisterns hewn out, which you did not hew, and vineyards and olive trees, which you did not plant, and when you eat and are full, then take heed lest you forget the Lord, who brought you out of the land of Egypt, out of the house of bondage. You shall fear the Lord your God; you shall serve him, and swear by his name. You shall not go after other gods, of the gods of the peoples who are round about you; for the Lord your God in the midst of you is a jealous God; lest the anger of the Lord your God be kindled against you, and he destroy you from off the face of the earth." (Deut. 6:4-15)

Give ear, O people, to my teaching;
  incline your ears to the words of my mouth!
I will open my mouth in a parable;
  I will utter dark sayings from of old,
things that we have heard and known,
  that our fathers have told us.
We will not hide them from their children,
  but tell to the coming generation
  the glorious deeds of the Lord, and his might,
  and the wonders which he has wrought.

He established a testimony in Jacob,
  and appointed a law in Israel,
  which he commanded our fathers
  to teach to their children;
that the next generation might know them,
  the children yet unborn,
and arise and tell them to their children
  so that they should set their hope in God,
and not forget the works of God,
  but keep his commandments;
and that they should not be like their fathers,
  a stubborn and rebellious generation,
a generation whose heart was not steadfast,
  whose spirit was not faithful to God.

The Ephraimites, armed with the bow,
  turned back on the day of battle.
They did not keep God's covenant,
  but refused to walk according to his law.
They forgot what he had done,
  and the miracles that he had shown them.
In the sight of their fathers he wrought marvels
  in the land of Egypt, in the fields of Zoan.

He divided the sea and let them pass through it,
    and made the waters stand like a heap.
In the daytime he led them with a cloud,
    and all the night with a fiery light.
He cleft rocks in the wilderness,
    and gave them drink abundantly as from the
        deep.
He made streams come out of the rock,
    and caused waters to flow down like rivers.

Yet they sinned still more against him,
    rebelling against the Most High in the desert.
They tested God in their heart
    by demanding the food they craved.
They spoke against God, saying,
    "Can God spread a table in the wilderness?
He smote the rock so that water gushed out
    and streams overflowed.
Can he also give bread,
    or provide meat for his people?"

Therefore, when the Lord heard, he was full of
      wrath;
    a fire was kindled against Jacob,
    his anger mounted against Israel;
because they had no faith in God,
    and did not trust his saving power.
Yet he commanded the skies above,
    and opened the doors of heaven;
and he rained down upon them manna to eat,
    and gave them the grain of heaven.
Man ate of the bread of the angels;
    he sent them food in abundance.
He caused the east wind to blow in the heavens,

and by his power he led out the south wind;
he rained flesh upon them like dust,
    winged birds like the sand of the seas;
he let them fall in the midst of their camp,
    all around their habitations.
And they ate and were well filled,
    for he gave them what they craved.
(Ps. 78:1-29)

Who has believed what we have heard?
    And to whom has the arm of the Lord been
        revealed?
For he grew up before him like a young plant,
    and like a root out of dry ground;
he had no form or comeliness that we should look at
        him,
    and no beauty that we should desire him.
He was despised and rejected by men;
    a man of sorrows, and acquainted with grief;
and as one from whom men hide their faces
    he was despised, and we esteemed him not.

Surely he has borne our griefs
    and carried our sorrows;
yet we esteemed him stricken,
    smitten by God, and afflicted.
But he was wounded for our transgressions,
    he was bruised for our iniquities;
upon him was the chastisement that made us
        whole,
    and with his stripes we are healed.
All we like sheep have gone astray;
    we have turned every one to his own way;
and the Lord has laid on him
    the iniquity of us all.

He was oppressed, and he was afflicted,
  yet he opened not his mouth;
like a lamb that is led to the slaughter,
  and like a sheep that before its shearers is dumb,
  so he opened not his mouth.
By oppression and judgment he was taken away;
  and as for his generation, who considered
that he was cut off out of the land of the living,
  stricken for the transgression of my people?
And they made his grave with the wicked
  and with a rich man in his death,
although he had done no violence,
  and there was no deceit in his mouth.

Yet it was the will of the Lord to bruise him;
  he has put him to grief;
when he makes himself an offering for sin,
  he shall see his offspring, he shall prolong his
    days;
the will of the Lord shall prosper in his hand;
  he shall see the fruit of the travail for his soul
    and be satisfied;
by his knowledge shall the righteous one, my
    servant,
  make many to be accounted righteous;
  and he shall bear their iniquities.
Therefore I will divide him a portion with the
    great,
  and he shall divide the spoil with the strong;
because he poured out his soul to death,
  and was numbered with the transgressors;
yet he bore the sin of many,
  and made intercession for the transgressors.
(Isa. 53:1-12)

## Confessions

*A confessional statement may be a silent prayer, a pastoral prayer, or a prayer printed in the order of worship which can be prayed in unison by the congregation.*

If my people, which are called by my name, shall humble themselves, and pray, and seek my face, and turn from their wicked ways; then will I hear from heaven, and will forgive their sin, and will heal their land. (2 Chron. 7:14, KJV)

Almighty God: in Jesus Christ you called us to be a servant people, but we do not do what you command. We are often silent when we should speak, and useless when we could be useful. We are lazy servants, timid and heartless, who turn neighbors away from your love. Have mercy on us, O God, and, though we do not deserve your care, forgive us, and free us from sin; through Jesus Christ our Lord. Amen. (From *The Worshipbook*, 1970, Presbyterian)

Have mercy on me, O God, according to thy
    steadfast love;
  according to thy abundant mercy blot out my
    transgressions.
Wash me thoroughly from my iniquity
  and cleanse me from my sin!

For I know my transgressions,
  and my sin is ever before me.
Against thee, thee only, have I sinned,
  and done that which is evil in thy sight,

so that thou art justified in thy sentence
   and blameless in thy judgment.
Behold, I was brought forth in iniquity,
   and in sin did my mother conceive me.

Behold, thou desirest truth in the inward being;
   therefore teach me wisdom in my secret heart.
(Ps. 51:1-6)

## Declarations of Pardon

Almighty God, our heavenly Father, who of thy
great mercy hast promised forgiveness of sins to all
them that with hearty repentance and true faith
turn to thee: Have mercy upon us; pardon and
deliver us from our sins; confirm and strengthen us
in all goodness; and bring us to everlasting life;
through Jesus Christ our Lord. Amen. (From *The
Book of Worship*, 1964, Methodist)

I waited patiently for the Lord;
   he inclined to me and heard my cry.
He drew me up from the desolate pit,
   out of the miry bog,
   and set my feet upon a rock,
   making my steps secure.
He put a new song in my mouth,
   a song of praise to our God.
Many will see and fear,
   and put their trust in the Lord.
(Ps. 40:1-3)

Who is in a position to condemn? Only Christ, and
Christ died for us, Christ rose for us, Christ reigns in
power for us, Christ prays for us. If a man is in

Christ, he becomes a new person altogether—the past is finished and gone, everything has become fresh and new. (From *The Worshipbook,* 1970, Presbyterian)

## "Sharing the Peace"

*The Lord's Supper is a fellowship meal, a communion of the saints. Opportunity needs to be provided for Christians to greet each other and even be reconciled to one another. The worship leader may instruct the congregation in whatever form of greeting may be appropriate—handshakes, hugs, kisses, hands held (even across church aisles)—while a fellowship hymn is sung.*

A new commandment I give unto you, That ye love one another; as I have loved you, that ye also love one another. By this shall all men know that ye are my disciples, if ye have love one to another. (John 13:34-35, KJV)

Greet one another with the kiss of love.
Peace to all of you that are in Christ. (1 Pet. 5:14)

Agree with one another, live in peace, and the God of love and peace will be with you. Greet one another with a holy kiss. (2 Cor. 13:11-12)

He who says he is in the Light and hates his brother is in the darkness still. He who loves his brother abides in the light, and in it there is no cause for stumbling. (1 John 2:9-10)

So if you are offering your gift at the altar, and there remember that your brother has something against you, leave your gift there before the altar and go; first be reconciled to your brother, and then come and offer your gift. (Matt. 5:23-24)

## New Testament Scripture Readings

And as they were eating, he took bread, and blessed, and broke it, and gave it to them, and said, "Take; this is my body." And he took the cup, and when he had given thanks he gave it to them and they all drank of it. And he said to them, "This is my blood of the covenant, which is poured out for many. Truly, I say to you, I shall not drink again of the fruit of the vine until that day when I drink it new in the kingdom of God." And when they had sung a hymn, they went out to the Mount of Olives. (Mark 14:22-26)

And when the hour came, he sat at table, and the apostles with him. And he said to them, "I have earnestly desired to eat this passover with you before I suffer; for I tell you I shall not eat it until it is fulfilled in the kingdom of God." And he took a cup, and when he had given thanks he said, "Take this, and divide it among yourselves; for I tell you that from now on I shall not drink of the fruit of the vine until the kingdom of God comes." And he took bread, and when he had given thanks he broke it and gave it to them, saying, "This is my body which is given for you. Do this in remembrance of me." And likewise the cup after supper, saying, "This cup which is poured out for you is the new covenant in my blood. (Luke 22:14-20)

For I received from the Lord what I also delivered to you, that the Lord Jesus on the night when he was betrayed took bread, and when he had given thanks, he broke it, and said, "This is my body which is for you. Do this in remembrance of me." In the same way also the cup, after supper, saying, "This cup is the new covenant in my blood. Do this, as often as you drink it, in remembrance of me." For as often as you eat this bread and drink the cup, you proclaim the Lord's death until he comes.

Whoever, therefore, eats the bread or drinks the cup of the Lord in an unworthy manner will be guilty of profaning the body and blood of the Lord. Let a man examine himself, and so eat of the bread and drink of the cup. (1 Cor. 11:23-28)

## Distribution of the Bread

*Normally, the bread or the cup is held until everyone is serving and after the prayer of thanksgiving is offered. If the worship leader is serving each participant individually, this guideline is, of course, excepted.*

This is that bread which came down from heaven: not as your fathers did eat manna, and are dead: he that eateth of this bread shall live for ever. (John 6:58, KJV)

Jesus said to them, "I am the bread of life; he who comes to me shall not hunger, and he who believes in me shall never thirst. (John 6:35)

So those who received his word were baptized, and there were added that day about three thousand souls. And they devoted themselves to the apostles' teaching and fellowship, to the breaking of bread and the prayers.

And fear came upon every soul; and many wonders and signs were done through the apostles. And all who believed were together and had all things in common; and they sold their possessions and goods and distributed them to all, as any had need. And day by day, attending the temple together and breaking bread in their homes, they partook of food with glad and generous hearts, praising God and having favor with all the people. And the Lord added to their number day by day those who were being saved. (Acts 2:41-47)

## Prayers of Thanksgiving—For the Bread

All glory is yours, Eternal God, who made the universe. We praise you for this earth, for life and breath, for beauty we have seen and wonders still to come. From the beginning, your living Word has guided and corrected us. Your prophets have called us from disobedience, and prepared us for the coming of your Son.

We praise you for the Christ, who, like us, yet lived among us full of grace and truth. For us he became poor and knew the sadness of our days; and for us he died on the cross and was buried. In Him, we know forgiveness and the lifting of burdens. He brings light to our darkness and opens our eyes to Your great glory. For, by faith, we believe that you raised and exalted Him, over all creation. And through the Holy Spirit we are heirs with Him of the promise of the fulness of life. Therefore, with thankful hearts we join the faithful of all times and places, praising your name and saying: Holy, Holy, God of power and majesty, Heaven and earth are full of your glory. O God Most High! (From *A Manual for Worship and Service,* 1976, Canadian Baptist)

Gracious Father, we thank you for the wonder of your acts of love, recalled for us in the 'good news' of the Gospel. We remember you, Lord Jesus, as you commanded, confident that we shall know you in the breaking of the bread. We remember you, O Christ, confident you will seal the bond of love in our hearts as we drink the cup. O Holy Spirit, who brought us here to proclaim the risen Lord, unite us in one body with Him who loved us and lived as 'the man for others' for us. (From *A Manual for Worship and Service,* 1976, Canadian Baptist)

We praise you, God our creator, for your good gifts to us and all mankind. We thank you for the friendship we have in Christ; and for the promise of your coming kingdom, where there will be no more hunger and thirst, and where man will be satisfied by your love. As this bread was once seed scattered on earth to be gathered into one loaf, so may your church be joined together into one holy people, who praise you for your love made known in Jesus Christ the Lord. (From *The Worshipbook,* 1970, Presbyterian)

Our Father, in the fullness of joy on the glorious resurrection day, we pause for a few moments of thoughtful communion around Thy table spread with the symbols of sacrifice.
Help us to understand that earth's saddest day, and earth's gladdest day were only one day apart. May we find in both days Thy prevailing love. Let this loaf appropriately remind us of the broken body of our suffering Lord. May these moments of communion quicken within us the spirit of humility, and

give us a sincere desire to show more love toward
Thee by unselfish service.

This we pray in the name of our Risen Redeemer,
even Jesus the Christ. Amen. (From *Minister's Service Manual,* 1958, Evangelical)

## Distribution of the Cup

Jesus said to them, "The cup that I drink you will
drink; and with the baptism with which I am baptized, you will be baptized." (Mark 10:39)

What shall I render to the Lord
  for all his bounty to me?
I will lift up the cup of salvation
  and call on the name of the Lord,
I will pay my vows to the Lord
  in the presence of all his people.
(Ps. 116:12-14)

Indeed, under the law almost everything is purified with blood, and without the shedding of blood
there is no forgiveness of sins. (Heb. 9:22)

## Prayers of Thanksgiving—For the Cup

Our Father, we read in Thy Word that without the
shedding of blood there can be no remission of sins.
As we take of the cup of suffering today may we be
reminded of Calvary and the supreme sacrifice made
by our Master upon the cross. Give us understanding
hearts and minds. Quicken within us the desire to
prove our sincerity as those who wear the name of
Christ and who desire to serve him consistently.

We would therefore together in this high moment

of worship renew our vows of loyalty to Thy Kingdom. Forgive us in our weaknesses. Strengthen us in
our noble purposes. This we pray in the name of
Christ our sinless Master. Amen. (From *Minister's
Service Manual,* 1958, Evangelical)

We thank you, Father, for this supper shared in
the Spirit with your Son Jesus, who makes us new
and strong, and brings us life eternal. We praise you
for giving all good gifts in him, and pledge ourselves
to serve you, even as you have served us in Jesus
Christ the Lord. Amen. (From *The Worshipbook,*
1970, Presbyterian)

We remember with thanksgiving those who have
loved and served thee in thy Church on earth, who
now rest from their labors (especially those most
dear to us, whom we name in our hearts before thee).
Keep us in fellowship with all thy saints, and bring
us at length to the joy of thy heavenly kingdom.
Grant this, O Father, for the sake of Jesus Christ,
our only mediator and advocate. Amen. (From *The
Book of Worship,* 1964, Methodist)

#### Hymn

*A fellowship hymn may be sung, or one of the
following biblical hymns may be read:*

I love the Lord, because he has heard
  my voice and my supplications.
Because he inclined his ear to me,
  therefore I will call on him as long as I live.
The snares of death encompassed me;
  the pangs of Sheol laid hold on me;
  I suffered distress and anguish.

Then I called on the name of the Lord:
  "O Lord, I beseech thee, save my life!"

Gracious is the Lord, and righteous;
  our God is merciful.
The Lord preserves the simple;
  when I was brought low, he saved me.
Return, O my soul, to your rest;
  for the Lord has dealt bountifully with you.

For thou hast delivered my soul from death,
  my eyes from tears,
  my feet from stumbling;
I walk before the Lord
  in the land of the living.
I kept my faith, even when I said,
  "I am greatly afflicted";
I said in my consternation,
  "Men are all a vain hope."

What shall I render to the Lord
  for all his bounty to me?
I will lift up the cup of salvation
  and call on the name of the Lord,
I will pay my vows to the Lord in the presence of all
    his people.
Precious in the sight of the Lord
  is the death of his saints.
O Lord, I am thy servant;
  I am thy servant, the son of thy handmaid.
  Thou hast loosed my bonds.
I will offer to thee the sacrifice of thanksgiving
  and call on the name of the Lord.
I will pay my vows to the Lord
  in the presence of all his people,

in the courts of the house of the Lord,
   in your midst, O Jerusalem.
Praise the Lord!
(Ps. 116:1-19)

Praise the Lord, all nations!
Extol him, all peoples!
For great is his steadfast love toward us;
   and the faithfulness of the Lord endures for ever.
Praise the Lord! (Ps. 117)

He is the image of the invisible God, the first-born
of all creation; for in him all things were created, in
heaven and on earth, visible and invisible, whether
thrones or dominions or principalities or authorities—all things were created through him and for
him. He is before all things, and in him all things
hold together. He is the head of the body, the church;
he is the beginning, the first-born from the dead,
that in everything he might be pre-eminent. For in
him all the fulness of God was pleased to dwell, and
through him to reconcile to himself all things,
whether on earth or in heaven, making peace by the
blood of his cross. (Col. 1:15-20)

### Notes

1. For an interesting theory of how this may have come about,
see Oscar Cullman and Franz J. Leenhardt, "The Meaning of the
Lord's Supper in Primitive Christianity," trans. J. G. Davies,
*Essays on the Lord's Supper* (Richmond: John Knox Press, 1958),
pp. 5-23.
2. At long last, well into my seminary career, I finally learned
why the tablecloth was placed on top of the Lord's Supper

elements rather than underneath. In the days before electricity and air conditioning, the upper tablecloth was used to keep off flies. Modern technology eliminated the need for the superfluous cloth, but tradition forgot why it was there, and it became part of the communion ritual in many churches.

3. Scholarly debate rages about whether or not the Last Supper was the Passover meal or preceded the Passover by a day. Whichever your persuasion, your church's celebration of the Lord's Supper service can be carried out in such a way as to educate your congregation regarding both your theology and chronology. Of course, the use of psalms of praise in worship is good theology at any time.

# 4
# The Christian Marriage Ceremony

The so-called Christian wedding is a prime target for reform!

The marriage ceremony is an occasion in the life of the church in which worship vies for preeminence with numerous traditions and customs, many of which are pagan in origin and practice. A certain amount of compromise is possible. The church has through the years "Christianized" and accepted some practices, including the giving and receiving of rings. But if the compromises are too many, or too extreme, or are not compromises at all but are no more than secular inroads into a Christian worship service, then the pastor should consider recommending a secular wedding to the couple desiring to be married.

Again, we need to be reminded of why we worship. We need to have God revealed to us, and we need to respond to God. We also need to witness to non-Christians about our Lord. Nonworship acts need to be removed from the Christian marriage ceremony. In the house of God, speaking on God's behalf, no convincing reason can be given for including words such as these: "Acting in the authority given to me by the laws of this state, I pronounce you husband and wife." In worship, a minister is acting by the authority vested in him or her by the laws and grace of God and the church, not the authority of the state. Join Will Campbell[1] in signing the legal documents before the worship period and be done with your civil duties. Once the worship service begins, let God, not the government, dominate.

Tradition is powerful and, when neutral in its moral or theological content, can be employed gainfully. But when tradition supplies us with erroneous forms and models, we need to be unrelenting in our efforts to establish new norms.

Worship manuals (such as this one), and books of forms (including the ancient *Book of Common Prayer*) are some of the chief culprits in giving legitimacy to questionable wedding habits. They might provide anywhere from one to five options for marriage rituals, and they leave little room for change within those few that are provided. Congregational involvement is rare or nonexistent. The emphasis is on the bride, the groom, the pastor, and "everything going without a hitch." I have been told by a wedding "director" that the event is a "show." Too often a climate for worship (and worship itself!) will have to be achieved against great odds. Anything short of major liturgical renewal in marriage worship services will be a frustratingly hit-and-miss effort.[2]

Since many brides, grooms, and parents will want to hold to many of the old forms, the pastor who is interested in the wedding being reformed to be a more meaningful worship experience needs to be prepared to refute or accommodate these requests on sound theological terms.[3] Simply changing methods without explanation would be a pastorally unwise action.

Pastor and participants in the wedding should ask initially why the ceremony is being held in the church, with the pastor presiding. History needs to be consulted for the answer. The fact is that marriages were not performed by ecclesiastical authorities or in buildings built for worship early in church history. Instead, they were secular events. However, the married couple often received some spiritual blessing or were prayed for by the village priest after the wedding ritual had already taken place in a home or a public building. But time passed, and apparently it was easier to provide only one person (the pastor) and one place (the church) to complete both the civil and spiritual matters surrounding the marriage. So the church inherited the wedding!

That historical fact has been a mixed blessing for pastors. Certainly in modern times, weddings provide an excellent forum to speak a word from God about the family—at a particularly crucial time in the lives of several individuals. The wedding brings with it a host of opportunities, which open the door to a host of motives. The occasion allows for the possibility of an evangelical word to the many non-Christians who come to the marriage ceremony of their Christian friends.

A pastoral or evangelical opportunity is often presented by the couple who are being married. The minister hopes to see a conversion, repentance, or improved Christian character during his or her counseling periods with the couple; *but,* when all is said and done, the pastor's words and the couple's vows may be a hypocritical mockery of what the pastor feels are the couple's true feelings and beliefs.

The social pressures surrounding weddings are immense. By the time that a pastor realizes that a Christian worship service is really improper for the uniting of a couple, it is "socially unacceptable" to refuse his own or the church's involvement. The invitations have already been sent out! Only careful pastoral planning will help prevent such a fiasco.

Repeatedly, in counseling, it should be emphasized that the wedding ceremony is a worship experience. Involve the couple, and possibly their families, in planning the liturgy. This will make the worship period more meaningful to them and their friends. Based on the couple's Christian commitment, or lack thereof, you can alter the service until it meets the anticipated congregation's needs for (1) revelation, (2) response, and (3) witness.

There are several potentially limiting factors in most wedding worship services. Organized choirs are hard to gather for an anthem. Unless there is a printed order of worship, and that is rare, litanies and confessions are limited to those to which the entire congregation has access in their hymnbooks or worshipbooks. Offerings and the entourage of worship elements that surround the offerings (prayers, doxologies, organ, or piano meditations) are absent in the wedding ceremony. The goal is a respectable and meaningful marriage service which gives due consideration to tradition but does not sacrifice its integrity as worship.

## Planning a Marriage Ceremony

The place to begin most worship services is with appropriate music, in this case establishing a joyful prelude (with organ music, a solo, or duet, etc.) to the events which will follow. A spoken call to worship is too seldom employed in weddings, but what better way is there to enlist the attention of all who are present and calm anxious nerves than to announce, "This is the day which the Lord has made;/let us rejoice and be glad in it" (Ps. 118:24)?

Scripture readings, from the Old Testament, the Gospels, and the Epistles, should be read. We can redeem our centuries of abuse of the Song of Solomon by reading it at weddings as a beautiful reminder that God created physical love.

After these traditional worship activities have been completed, we can incorporate what is usually the initial part of the wedding ceremony, often beginning, "Dearly Beloved." What this is, simply, is instruction in the Christian faith. It usually takes the form of a defense of marriage being a Christian institution, incorporating arguments from the Old Testament, from the life of Jesus, and from the teachings of Paul. Depending on circumstances, it is possible for the gospel to be proclaimed here. The pastor could easily relate the beginnings of a marriage to the new birth of a Christian and tell the good news of Christ in an effective way.

Certainly one of the meaningful hymns of the Christian faith or a hymn about the family (not just a solo about love) would involve the congregation and keep them from simply being spectators. The very least that can be done is to have the congregation join in saying the Lord's Prayer together.

Somewhere in this portion of the service, most weddings insert the custom of the father giving away the bride. This has more dangers inherent than any other single part of the "traditional" service, but, with work, even this custom is salvageable. Why do only the bride's parents give their child away? Why does just the father normally give the daughter away? And do we really mean "give her away"? This sounds like the bride is the possession of the parents, and though they are too sophisticated to sell her, as they would in some societies, they retain the right to "give her away."

Of course there are many redeeming values in the tradition of involving the parents in the wedding ceremony, and there should be no intrinsic objection to one parent representing all four, just as a public prayer speaks to God on behalf of the entire congregation in a Lord's Day worship service. The parents, though they do not "own" their children, have invested a major portion of their lives in their children's upbringing. They "deserve" an opportunity to be involved in this worship period as more than observers. Also, the Bible expounds a very clear concept that the child is to leave his or her parents and to cling to the marriage partner. This portion of the service would do well to celebrate (or at least mark) this important life passage. It would involve all parents, though one can be the spokesperson for the rest. I believe that some "in-law" problems might be settled if the parents of the bride and groom were asked to consider this commitment before the worship service and agree to give a proper public response to their

Christian obligations in this matter.

In marrying persons who have children by a previous marriage, I like to involve the children in the wedding ceremony and ask for their blessing.

Next, the minister charges the couple and speaks on behalf of God and the church. The couple should be challenged to a mutual commitment of service. The charge should reflect Christian standards for specific circumstances. I am impressed by the pastor's explanation to the timid groom who wanted the ceremony to be simplified and shortened. The groom only wanted to be required to say that he was now "in love" with his bride. The pastor commented that everyone knew that already. The important question was, "How will you love her? Will you love her when she is sick, or old, or cranky? Your God and your church think that these questions are vital."

The responses of the couple reflect that they are still "single," not yet one mind, one body, and one spirit. They answer these charges as individuals. Their answers constitute the dedication of the groom and the dedication of the bride. The bride and groom in fact marry each other. This act is between them and God, while the church acts as a witness. These dedications are usually called vows. The charges and the vows should reflect a commitment of each to serve the partner with body, mind, and soul. These vows should be more than poetry. They should be substantive and do more than hint at the covenant that is being established. To repeat, the vows should indicate specific commitments that the couple is making, one to the other.

The charge and the dedications are usually divided into two parts, with the ring exchange constituting the second set of vows. The ring ceremony has become almost sacramental in its importance, a symbol as rich in its imagery to many as baptism.

Though vows are normally spoken between the bride and

groom, they may include a new or renewed commitment by the couple to God, the church, or their families. Or the dedication may also be by the church or the family to the couple. Such a practice would add an important social dimension to the marriage service.

After the vows have been exchanged, the pastor, or a friend of the couple, may lead in a prayer of thanksgiving and intercession for the bride and groom. Such a prayer might include mention of the parents, churches, teachers, and friends who have been instrumental in the lives of the couple. It might ask for all of the married couples present to share a renewed sense of commitment to their own marriages. The prayer is a place where the pastor should make a distinct effort to personalize the worship service if he or she has not already done so.

Next in the ceremony would come the "Declaration of Marriage." The minister pronounces that in the sight of God and the church (which must be represented by the gathered witnesses), the couple is now married. I am for forever deleting any reference to the state from the declaration of marriage. Because of common-law marriage regulations, enough ambiguity exists to keep dozens of lawyers busy for years arguing about the exact point at which a couple is married in the eyes of most states. Leave the state to its own devices. Instead, declare that in the eyes of God, the couple is now married.

In conjunction with this pronunciation, another charge is customary. However stated, it usually reflects the sentiment of Matthew 19:6: "What therefore God has joined together, let not man put asunder."

A doxology or benediction would conclude the spoken portion of the worship service.

Beware of the tradition of telling the groom that he may kiss the bride. Some ministers outlaw the practice altogether. Others allow it as a token of Christian affection but "warn" the couple in counseling to keep the kiss short, sweet, and sanitary. If you have ever had to endure a long, passionate kiss just a foot in front of you while the congregation became uncomfortable watching the honeymoon begin, you would agree that the quicker this part of the ritual is over, the better off you and the congregation are.

Sometimes a couple may want to do something out of the ordinary at their wedding. At least it may be unusual to you and your church. Prayer, biblical and theological reflection, and the maturity or wisdom of the couple might all be factors in deciding what to do.

Celebrating the Lord's Supper is a community affair. It would never be appropriate to let the congregation watch the couple celebrate Communion alone. The problem with offering the elements to all of the guests at a wedding is that there will surely be some non-Christians present. Does the couple want the pastor to "interrupt" the service for a quick lesson on who may partake of the elements and another lesson on what the bread and the cup symbolize?

A popular symbolic act is the lighting of one candle by the couple from two separate candles to represent the union that takes place in marriage where two persons become one. If it is meaningful to the couple, then this may be an excellent conclusion to the worship period.

Any number of worship elements not mentioned above might be effectively included in a marriage worship service if the pastor, the couple, and the church so desire, and if the resources are available.

A wedding might be ordered in this way:

Prelude
Call to Worship
Old Testament Scripture Readings
Affirmation of Marriage
Hymn
Blessing of the Parents

New Testament Scripture Readings
Wedding Vows
The Ring Ceremony
Wedding Prayer
Declaration of Marriage
Benediction
Holy Kiss
Recessional

## Calls to Worship

I will give thanks to the Lord with my whole heart;
   I will tell of all thy wonderful deeds.
I will be glad and exult in thee,
   I will sing praise to thy name, O Most High.
(Ps. 9:1-2)

Lord, thou hast been our dwelling place
   in all generations.
Before the mountains were brought forth,
   or ever thou hadst formed the earth and the world,
   from everlasting to everlasting thou art God.
(Ps. 90:1-2)

Make a joyful noise unto the Lord, all ye lands.
Serve the Lord with gladness: come before his presence with singing. Know ye that the Lord he is God: it is he that hath made us, and not we ourselves; we are his people, and the sheep of his pasture. Enter into his gates with thanksgiving, and into his courts with praise: be thankful unto him, and bless his name. For the Lord is good; his mercy is everlasting; and his truth endureth to all generations. (Ps. 100, KJV)

This is the day which the Lord hath made; we will

rejoice and be glad in it. (Ps. 118:24, KJV)

## Old Testament Scripture Readings

*Any of the following passages of Scripture would be appropriate for a wedding:*

So the Lord caused a deep sleep to fall upon the man, and while he slept took one of his ribs and closed up its place with flesh; and the rib which the Lord God had taken from the man he made into a woman and brought her to the man. Then the man said,
"This at last is bone of my bones
   and flesh of my flesh;
she shall be called Woman,
   because she was taken out of Man."
Therefore a man leaves his father and his mother and cleaves to his wife, and they become one flesh. (Gen. 2:21-24)

"Entreat me not to leave you or to return from following you; for where you go I will go, and where you lodge I will lodge; your people shall be my people, and your God my God; where you die I will die, and there will I be buried. May the Lord do so to me and more also if even death parts me from you." (Ruth 1:16-17)

Two are better than one, because they have a good reward for their toil. For if they fall, one will lift up his fellow; but woe to him who is alone when he falls and has not another to lift him up. Again, if two lie together, they are warm; but how can one be warm alone? And though a man might prevail against one who is alone, two will withstand him. A threefold cord is not quickly broken. (Eccl. 4:9-12)

My beloved speaks and says to me:
"Arise, my love, my fair one,
    and come away;
for lo, the winter is past,
    the rain is over and gone.
The flowers appear on the earth,
    the time of singing has come,
and the voice of the turtledove
    is heard in our land.
The fig tree puts forth its figs,
    and the vines are in blossom;
    they give forth fragrance.
Arise, my love, my fair one,
    and come away.
O my dove, in the clefts of the rock,
    in the covert of the cliff,
let me see your face,
    let me hear your voice,
for your voice is sweet,
    and your face is comely.
Catch us the foxes,
    the little foxes,
that spoil the vineyards,
    for our vineyards are in blossom.

My beloved is mine and I am his,
    he pastures his flock among the lilies.
Until the day breathes
    and the shadows flee,
turn, my beloved, be like a gazelle,
    or a young stag upon rugged mountains.
(Song of Sol. 2:10-17)

## Affirmations of Marriage

_____ (Bride), _____ (Groom) and Family and Friends.

We are gathered here today because Christians believe in marriage. We believe that it is appropriate for Christians to gather to celebrate this happy occasion and to praise God for his goodness. Even more importantly, we believe that it is right to make our marriage vows to one another in the presence of God and his people. We cannot act alone, even if we so desire. Each of us is the result of the influences of family and friends, of many years of interaction with other people. When we gather for a Christian wedding ceremony, we simply acknowledge that God and other people have touched and affected our lives in significant ways.

The Bible is full of reminders that God established the home, and that he gives his blessing to those people who follow the simple guidelines that he has set forth. We leave our parents and cling to our spouse. We commit ourselves to his or her well-being. We remain faithful physically, emotionally, and spiritually to the person whom we have freely chosen to marry. This is the word of God for Christians who are married.

We are gathered together today, in the presence of God, and in the company of you friends, to join together this man, _____ (Groom), and this woman, _____ (Bride), in God's Holy institution of marriage.

We all should know, and _____ (Groom) and _____ (Bride) do know, I am assured, that marriage is not to be entered into lightly or unadvisedly, but reverently, not only with the joy and hope of Christians, but also in awe of God whose will they shall seek to follow.

The chief word, as we look at a biblical perspective of marriage, is not love but *commitment*: a commitment of *life*.

In a Christian marriage (and we expect no less), there must first exist a total allegiance to Jesus Christ and his will. Only after this commitment with God is sealed can I, as a Christian minister, be satisfied that these two people can effectively commit themselves to one another.

It is necessary to understand that God, not man, designed marriage. In the quiet of the garden of Eden, before evil had touched the world, God saw that it was not good for the man to be alone. He made a partner suitable for him, two persons complimenting and corresponding to one another, and established the rite of marriage.

We must emphasize the importance of what will take place in the uniting of these two persons. Marriage is the foundation of home life and social order and must remain so until the end of time. It was sanctioned and honored by our Lord Jesus Christ. So it happens that a man shall leave his father and mother, and cleave unto his wife; and the two shall become one flesh.

Dearly beloved, we are gathered together here in the sight of God, and in the face of this company, to join together this Man and this Woman in holy Matrimony; which is an honourable estate, instituted of God, signifying unto us the mystical union that is betwixt Christ and his Church: which holy

estate Christ adorned and beautified with his presence and first miracle that he wrought in Cana of
Galilee, and is commended of Saint Paul to be
honourable among all men: and therefore is not by
any to be entered into unadvisedly or lightly; but
reverently, discreetly, advisedly, soberly, and in the
fear of God. Into this holy estate these two persons
present come now to be joined. If any man can show
just cause, why they may not lawfully be joined
together, let him now speak, or else hereafter for
ever hold his peace. (From *The Book of Common
Prayer,* 1790, Anglican)

A wedding is that occasion when a man and a
woman publicly proclaim their love and declare their
commitment to one another. By its very nature it is
both a solemn and a happy event. For some of you
gathered here, this ceremony will prompt a flood of
personal memories, for others of you it will set in
motion dreams and aspirations. For all of us it will be a
sharing in a most intimate and love-filled moment in
the lives of two people we know and appreciate. But for
_____ and _____ who stand here before us, this
ceremony will be an act of participation in what they
believe to be God's will for their lives.

They are both pleased and honoured that you have
responded to their invitation to share these happy
and sacred moments with them and are prayerful
that the blessing of the Lord Our God will be upon us
as we assemble here. (From *A Manual for Worship
and Service,* 1976, Canadian Baptist)

## Blessings of the Parents

PASTOR: The idea of a father "giving his daughter
away" seems archaic today. But the principle under-

lying that ancient statement is still valid. The Book of Genesis tells us that "a man leaves his father and mother and cleaves to his wife, and they become one flesh." When a father agrees to "give his daughter away," he is endorsing this biblical principle, and giving his consent to his daughter's marriage to this man. By his agreement, he willingly forfeits the primary place that he and his wife have had in his daughter's life, and gives his blessing to the marriage of his daughter and her husband.

With that understanding, I am prepared to ask, "Who gives this woman to be married to this man?"
PARENT OF THE BRIDE: I do.

FATHER OF THE BRIDE: Her mother and I do.

PASTOR: Who gives this woman to be married to this man?
PARENT: I do.

PASTOR: Will the father of the bride please present her to the Groom?

PASTOR: Do you give your blessing to _____ (Bride) and _____ (Groom) in their new relationship? Do you support them with your love and wisdom? At the same time, do you promise to allow them the freedom to grow through their own experiences?
PARENTS: We do.

PASTOR: _____ (Bride) is about to pledge her faith, love and loyalty to _____ (Groom). Is there one of her family who is prepared to present her to him?

FATHER OR OTHER DESIGNATE: "I commit
_____ (Bride) into your love and care. May God
bless you richly." (From *A Manual for Worship and
Service*, 1976, Canadian Baptist)

## The Blessing of the Children

*Obviously, this worship element would apply only
in circumstances where one of the marriage partners
has children by a previous marriage.*

In most weddings, the parents are asked to release
their children and to give the marriage their blessing.

Today, however, we're going to ask these children
to give their blessing to their parents.

_____ (Bride) and _____ (Groom) will need
your support to have their marriage be as happy and
as strong as it might be. Do you children promise to
support them and their marriage?

Children: We do.

## New Testament Scripture Readings

If I speak in the tongues of men and of angels, but
have not love, I am a noisy gong or a clanging cym-
bal. And if I have prophetic powers, and understand
all mysteries and all knowledge, and if I have all
faith, so as to remove mountains, but have not love, I
am nothing. If I give away all I have, and if I deliver
my body to be burned, but have not love, I gain
nothing.

Love is patient and kind; love is not jealous or
boastful; it is not arrogant or rude. Love does not
insist on its own way; it is not irritable or resentful;
it does not rejoice at wrong, but rejoices in the right.

Love bears all things, believes all things, hopes all things, endures all things.

Love never ends; as for prophecies, they will pass away; as for tongues, they will cease; as for knowledge, it will pass away. For our knowledge is imperfect and our prophecy is imperfect; but when the perfect comes, the imperfect will pass away. When I was a child, I spoke like a child, I thought like a child, I reasoned like a child; when I became a man, I gave up childish ways. For now we see in a mirror dimly, but then face to face. Now I know in part; then I shall understand fully, even as I have been fully understood. So faith, hope, love abide, these three; but the greatest of these is love. (1 Cor. 13:1-13)

Be subject to one another out of reverence for Christ. Wives, be subject to your husbands, as to the Lord. For the husband is the head of the wife as Christ is the head of the church, his body, and is himself its Savior. As the church is subject to Christ, so let wives also be subject in everything to their husbands. Husbands, love your wives, as Christ loved the church and gave himself up for her. (Eph. 5:21-25)

Have this mind among yourselves, which is yours in Christ Jesus, who, though he was in the form of God, did not count equality with God a thing to be grasped, but emptied himself, taking the form of a servant, being born in the likeness of men. And being found in human form he humbled himself and became obedient unto death, even death on a cross. Therefore God has highly exalted him and bestowed on him the name which is above every name, that at the name of Jesus every knee should bow, in heaven and on earth and under the earth, and every tongue confess that Jesus Christ is Lord, to the glory of God the Father. (Phil. 2:5-11)

## Wedding Vows

PASTOR: _____ (Groom) do you promise to live with _____ (Bride) according to God's purposes? Do you promise to commit yourself to meeting her needs: physical, emotional, and spiritual? Do you promise that, whatever the circumstances, you will love, honor, and sustain her, and that, as long as you both shall live, you will be faithful to her? Do you so promise?

GROOM: I do.

PASTOR: _____ (Bride) do you promise to live with _____ (Groom) according to God's purposes? Do you promise to commit yourself to meeting his needs: physical, emotional, and spiritual? Do you promise that, whatever the circumstances, you will love, honor, and sustain him, and that, as long as you both shall live, you will be faithful to him? Do you so promise?

BRIDE: I do.

PASTOR: Will you, _____ (Groom), take _____ (Bride) to be your wife? Will you promise before God and these friends to be her faithful husband, to share with her in plenty and in want, in joy and sorrow, in sickness and in health, to forgive and strengthen her, and to join with her so that together you may serve God and others as long as you both shall live?

GROOM: I will.

PASTOR: Will you, _____ (Bride), take _____ (Groom) to be your husband? Will you promise before God and these friends to be his faithful wife, to share with him in plenty and in want, in joy and sorrow, in sickness and in health, to forgive and strengthen him, and to join with him so that together you may serve God and others as long as you both shall live?

BRIDE: I will.

PASTOR: _____ (Groom) Wilt thou have this Woman to thy wedded wife, to live together after God's ordinance in the holy estate of Matrimony? Wilt thou love her, comfort her, honour, and keep her in sickness and in health; and, forsaking all others, keep thee only unto her, so long as ye both shall live?

GROOM: I will.

PASTOR: _____ (Bride) Wilt thou have this Man to thy wedded husband, to live together after God's ordinance in the holy estate of Matrimony? Wilt thou love him, comfort him, honour, and keep him in sickness and in health; and, forsaking all others, keep thee only unto him, so long as ye both shall live?

BRIDE: I will. (From *The Book of Common Prayer,* 1790, Anglican)

PASTOR: You _____ (Bride) and you _____ (Groom) having come to me signifying your desire to be formally united in marriage, and being assured that no legal, moral, or religious barriers hinder this proper union, I command you to join your right hands and give heed to the question now asked you.

_____ (Groom) In taking the woman whom you hold by the right hand to be your lawful and wedded wife, I require you to promise to love and cherish her, to honor and sustain her, in sickness as in health, in poverty as in wealth, in the bad that may darken your days, in the good that may light your ways, and to be true to her in all things until death alone shall part you.

Do you so promise?

GROOM: I do.

PASTOR: _____ (Bride) In taking the man who holds you by the right hand to be your lawful and wedded husband, I require you to promise to love and cherish him, to honor and sustain him, in sickness as in health, in poverty as in wealth, in the bad that may darken your days, in the good that may light your ways, and to be true to him in all things until death alone shall part you.

Do you so promise?

BRIDE: I do. (From *The Pastor's Manual,* 1934, Southern Baptist)

## The Ring Ceremony

The ring is a material symbol that has been designed to illustrate a spiritual truth.

A ring has two characteristics which make it suitable as a reminder to us of the importance of keeping Christ in our marriages.

First, the ring is a circle. Circles never end. Christian marriages should never end. They should last and last and last. Difficult times will come, but the commitment of Christians is to make their marriage go on forever. The ring, which is a circle, is a reminder of that never-ending commitment.

Also, rings are made out of a precious metal, usually silver or gold, which has the unusual quality of getting better and more valuable with age. Instead of wearing out and deteriorating, we pray for your love to grow and improve with age.

With these characteristics of your rings in mind, I ask you to exchange rings with one another.

PASTOR: _____ (Groom), do you give this ring to _____ (Bride) as a sign of your Christian commitment to her in marriage?

GROOM: I do.

PASTOR: _____ (Bride), do you give this ring to _____ (Groom) as a sign of your Christian commitment to him in marriage?

BRIDE: I do.

PASTOR: The ring is like a string around your finger. It reminds you of something. It is a symbol, a sign. Every time that you see your wedding ring, you will be reminded of the commitment that you made to one another here today.

GROOM: I give you this ring as a sign of our love and commitment.

BRIDE: I give you this ring as a sign of our love and commitment.

The wedding ring is the outward and visible sign of an inward and spiritual grace, signifying to all the uniting of this man and woman in holy matrimony, through the Church of Jesus Christ our Lord.

Let us pray.

Bless, O Lord, the giving of these rings, that they who wear them may abide in thy peace, and continue in thy favor; through Jesus Christ our Lord. Amen.

*The minister shall then deliver the proper ring to the man to put upon the third finger of the woman's left hand. The man, holding the ring there, shall say after the minister,*

In token and pledge of our constant faith and

abiding love, with this ring I thee wed, in the name
of the Father, and of the Son, and of the Holy Spirit.
Amen.

*Then, if there is a second ring, the minister shall
deliver it to the woman to put upon the third finger of
the man's left hand; and the woman, holding the ring
there, shall say after the minister,*

In token and pledge of our constant faith and
abiding love, with this ring I thee wed, in the name
of the Father, and of the Son, and of the Holy Spirit.
Amen. (From *The Book of Worship,* 1964, Methodist)

## Wedding Prayers

O God of Love, Thou hast established marriage for
the welfare and happiness of mankind. Now the joys
of _____ (Bride) and _____ (Groom) will be
doubled since the happiness of one is the happiness
of the other. Their burdens will be halved since they
now will share them.

Bless this husband. May he so live that she may
find in him the heaven for which her heart truly
longs.

Bless this wife. Give her that inner beauty of soul
that never fades, that eternal youth that is found in
holding fast to the things that never age.

Give them a great spiritual purpose in life. May
they seek first the Kingdom of God and His righteousness. Loving Thee best, they shall love each
other more, and faithful unto Thee, faithful to each
other they will be.

May they not expect that perfection of each other
that belongs only to Thee.

Now make such assignments to them on the scroll

of Thy will as will bless them and will develop their character as they walk together. Give them enough tears to keep them tender, enough hurts to keep them human, enough failure to keep their hands clenched tightly to Thine, and enough success to make them sure they walk with God. May they never take each other's love for granted but always experience that breathless wonder which exclaims that out of all the world, "You have chosen me!"

Then when life is done and the sun is setting, may they be found then as now, still hand in hand, still thanking God for each other. May they serve Thee happily, faithfully together until at last one shall lay the other in Thine arms.

This we ask through Jesus Christ, great lover of our souls. Amen. (Anonymous)

Holy, Righteous, and Merciful Father, alike Creator, Preserver, and Redeemer of mankind, fill these thy servants with a deep sense of the solemn obligations which they have just assumed. Guide them to look to thee for grace in their efforts to discharge these obligations with honor to themselves, in thy sight and in the sight of man. Ordain that their love now mutually pledged may never falter whatever course life may take with them. Crown their lives with lovingkindness and tender mercies, and provide for their protection while they travel the uneven way that leads from now to the end. . . . Lead them into the fulness of spiritual understanding and holy living, that they may have an abundant entrance into the joys everlasting. So we pray through Jesus Christ our Lord. (From *The Pastor's Manual,* 1934, Southern Baptist)

God of love and faithfulness, _____ and _____ have just committed themselves to undertake the most solemn and sacred obligation known to mankind. We who have witnessed and participated in this ceremony are conscious of their needs for Your grace and help as they seek honourably and lovingly to fulfill their commitments. We pray, therefore, that the love that they have mutually pledged may be so enriched by Your love that it may never falter or grow cold, no matter what their life experiences. May the wisdom and insight which is now theirs be enhanced by the wisdom from above, that they might clearly discern and choose the right path for living. May the strength and endurance of Your Holy Spirit not only offer to them protection on their course of life, but also afford them the spiritual and physical resources they will require in their daily pursuit of love, happiness and fulfilment. As You have so faithfully and effectively communicated love, understanding, forgiveness, trust and hope, we pray that You will be the ever present Teacher and Helper as _____ (Bride) and _____ (Groom) seek to communicate with each other. Grant to them, we pray, the qualities of kindness, mercy, honesty, openness and love in their relationship with each other and with all others.

May the home they establish be blessed with peace, and the family that may be added to them know physical and spiritual well-being. May spiritual understanding and holy living be their inheritance.

May Your grace, mercy and peace be a part of their lives from this day forward, through Jesus Christ Our Lord. Amen. (From *A Manual for Worship and*

*Service,* 1976, Canadian Baptist)

*The pastor or a friend may lead in a more person-
alized prayer for the couple being united.*

## Declarations of Marriage

_____ (Bride) and _____ (Groom), since you
have committed yourselves to a lifelong love, before
God and these witnesses, and since you have agreed
to meet the needs of each other as long as you both
live, and you have made your intentions public,
acting in the authority vested in me by God and his
church, I now pronounce you husband and wife.
"What therefore God has joined together, let not man
put asunder."

Forasmuch as _____ and _____ have cove-
nanted together in marriage and have declared the
same before God and in the presence of this company, I pronounce them Husband and Wife, in the
Name of the Father, and of the Son, and of the Holy
Ghost. Amen.
"What therefore God has joined together, let not
man put asunder."

## Benedictions

The Lord bless you and keep you:
The Lord make his face to shine upon you, and be
    gracious to you:
The Lord lift up his countenance upon you, and
    give you peace (Num. 6:24-26). Amen.

May the God of steadfastness and encouragement
grant you to live in such harmony with one another,

in accord with Christ Jesus, that together you may with one voice glorify the God and Father of our Lord Jesus Christ. (Rom. 15:5-6) Amen.

Grace, mercy, and peace from God the Father and Christ Jesus our Lord. (2 Tim. 1:2) Amen.

Grace be with you, mercy, and peace, from God the Father, and from the Lord Jesus Christ, the Son of the Father, in truth and love. (2 John 1:3, KJV) Amen.

## Notes

1. Will D. Campbell, *Brother to a Dragonfly* (New York: The Seabury Press, 1979).
2. Some problems can be handled by a church providing a mimeographed "Wedding Policy" which has been approved by the official board or the congregation. This policy can remind the couple that the church is neither a garden (therefore flowers should be limited) nor a gymnasium (so pulpit furniture should not be obscured).
3. Once a pastor has established a theology of worship for weddings which is accessible in some form (mimeograph, book, or whatever) to the couple, the "burden of proof" for change should be with them, not the minister.

# 5
# The Funeral Service

Funerals are doubtless the single most difficult aspect of a minister's duties. Pastors are called on to say something to comfort a bereaved family when they themselves may be grieving. Families in mourning often have unreasonable wishes: they want assurance that their non-Christian relative is in heaven; they want a "brief" funeral service, yet invite three ministers to participate; they want only a graveside service "because it's easier for everybody," but they want a full-length sermon "because Mama loved to hear you preach so much." Decision making about funeral arrangements is often difficult for the pastor.

The minister must decide whether to treat the funeral service as a worship service or simply as a tradition which may or may not have any relationship to the worship of God. Certainly, sometimes the potential for worship is minimal, especially when the deceased was not a Christian nor are his or her family or friends who are in attendance.

Still, the three purposes of worship apply. The funeral service is an opportunity to have God revealed to the bereaved, to give the family and friends of the deceased an opportunity to respond to the revelation of God, and to witness to the good news of Jesus Christ. To console or comfort friends is *not* the reason we worship. However, experience has shown that worship services (which we call funerals) at the deaths of our friends when we hear about God do comfort us. So, usually, our foremost concern in a funeral is to provide for the congregation a revelation from or about God.

There is nothing intrinsically wrong with witnessing to non-Christians or calling Christians to some kind of response at funerals, but centuries of practice have indicated that grief-stricken people have their "response mechanisms" dulled somewhat by their grief in what someone has called "emotional anesthesia." This state of mind is expressed in a sluggishness of spirit which either responds poorly to any stimuli or which unthinkingly overreacts and is easily manipulated. Thus you may have heard of a sermon preached at a service following the tragic death of a teenager at which dozens or even hundreds of persons responded by "walking down the aisle" after an evangelistic invitation.

Standard and honorable practice at funerals ordinarily is to limit opportunities for response to the very familiar. The Apostles' Creed or the Lord's Prayer spoken in unison, the twenty-third Psalm read responsively, or a favorite hymn sung by the congregation are examples of familiar responses.

Using a funeral service for evangelistic purposes is an acceptable but problematic course of action. On occasion this request may come to you from the family of the deceased. Certainly, in most congregations ever assembled for a funeral, there are non-Christians, candidates for evangelism. To many pastors, the temptation to preach evangelistically to their "largest congregation of the year" is too great to resist. One word of caution: if you do decide to witness at a funeral service, be careful to present the responsibilities as well as privileges of the Christian life and avoid manipulation of the hearers. A method of evangelism at funerals which seems to me to have integrity is to let the character of the deceased be mentioned as testimony to the Christian life.

Still, achieving thoughtful responses at funerals is more often the exception and not the rule. The rule is that a funeral is a place to talk about Almighty God, the Creator, the Sustainer of life, the Redeemer, the Holy One, the Judge, the Compassionate Father, ad infinitum. When we stand before death, we are awed, we are mystified, we are wounded, and we are humbled. We realize that we are finite, and we become aware of the Infinite.

It is out of the many experiences of the pastor with the individual, with the family, and with the church and the community that the minister will know which attribute(s) or law(s) of God or of God's creation to emphasize. In some cases, the emphasis will be on God as Friend (of the deceased). In other instances, the emphasis will be on the Holy Spirit as Comforter (of the family). With some families, the finality of the death of the body must be explained. With others, the stress of the pastor's words should be on the resurrection.

## Planning a Funeral

Because the family and many friends will be experiencing the emotional anesthesia mentioned earlier, and because funerals are often held in the afternoon when many people are naturally drowsy, wisdom would seem to dictate a brief worship service. Lack of preparation time also would normally indicate a shorter worship service than the Lord's Day worship would ordinarily be. It is better to have a brief service, well planned and well executed, than a longer, poorly-prepared liturgy. If there is not ample time to rehearse the choir for an anthem, or a trio for a hymn, then it is better not to have it. If there is not time to give some thought to and perhaps to write a prayer of confession (or whatever) beforehand, then possibly the Lord's Prayer or a short and simple extemporaneous prayer should be spoken instead. Litanies or responsive readings may be used, but there is usually little time for original preparation. Necessity usually makes the funeral service brief, especially if it includes well-prepared remarks by the pastor.

There is no worship principle which affects whether the pastor leads the bereaved family into the sanctuary or whether the minister comes in from a side door as is usual on the Lord's Day. Funeral directors can be expected to give the family all of the immediate assistance that they need in being seated. The pastor should motion for the congregation to stand (as a sign of respect) when the family enters the sanctuary.

A funeral worship service, like any other gathering for worship, may include a call to worship. Scripture readings, anthems, hymns, and prayers would normally precede any meditation or sermon that will be given. Since a funeral usually has only one worship leader, I have found it helpful to have an organ meditation or hymn immediately before my remarks, which allows me time to recollect my thoughts. Obituaries (a biographical sketch of the deceased) or eulogies (speech in praise of the deceased) should be avoided unless they contribute to the worship experience. Though we should not try to (and cannot) preach someone into heaven, I believe that the individual whose funeral it is at least deserves to have his or her name mentioned. Always mention it with integrity: don't say more than you ought, but try to say something. As some folks jokingly remark, they want to be sure they are at the right funeral!

The initial part of the worship service may be held in the church, the home, or a funeral parlor or chapel. For Christians, the church is preferable, for that is their most familiar place of corporate worship. (If the service is at the graveside only, that most often indicates that the family desires a brief service; so a condensed version of worship should be employed.) The pastor needs to provide both a proper terminus of worship for those who will not be going to the graveside, and a continuity for those who will be. A benediction may be said from the pulpit, after which the pastor should motion for the congregation to rise while leading the processional from the church building. A principle does apply here to the pastor's actions in this "interim" period. The principle is that the graveside service is a continuation of the service in the sanctuary and the mood should be maintained. If the sanctuary part of the service is triumphant, as it would ordinarily be for a Christian, then the interment should not become a somber reversal of mood. Also the pastor's actions and words during the interval between the two parts of the funeral service should be consistent with actions and words during the actual worship period. Joking with friends and discussing business with church officers can wait until after the graveside worship is completed. Staying with the family and the "funeral party" (most often in front of the casket) allows the pastor to be the "signal" to those in attendance at the graveside that the worship service is recommencing and that their conversations should cease.

History and local customs have provided many options at the graveside. In some instances, the church has completed its duties in the church sanctuary, and Christian ministers have not participated at the graveside. In other times and places, the Lord's Supper has been served to the congregation at the graveside.

Most denominations which have structured liturgies have brief and simple interment services, consisting of Scripture, a prayer, a statement of the committal of the body to the ground, and a benediction. Beware of commending the soul to God, for that is an act which the theology of most Protestants would not allow, deeming the commendation "too late" to be effective or meaningful.

Funerals for outstanding Christians should have a distinctively different character from funerals for notorious pagans.

Certainly the task of making such judgments is filled with dangers, but uniform treatment of religiously diverse people is too high a price to pay for standardization of liturgy. The minimum that we can do as pastors for unbelievers is to read Scripture and have prayer. That at least affords the opportunity to have God revealed to those present and lets the pastor respond to God on their behalf, if they are unwilling or unable to respond for themselves.

Most areas, even some churches within the same area, have different funeral customs. Every person in a new pastorate would be well advised to confer with one (or more—for often opinions and memories are different) of his or her senior deacons or elders and one or more local funeral directors to discover traditions and customs peculiar to that locale.

A typical funeral service for Christians might be designed like this:

Prelude
Call to Worship
Old Testament Reading(s)
Prayer of Thanksgiving
Congregational Hymn
New Testament Reading(s)
Sermon
Benediction
Recessional
(at Graveside)
New Testament Reading
The Lord's Prayer
Committal
Benediction

A funeral service for a non-Christian would emphasize Scripture and prayer:

Prelude
Call to Worship
Old Testament Readings
Prayer of Confession
Organ Meditation
Selected Poetry
New Testament Readings
Benediction
Recessional
(at Graveside)
Call to Prayer
Prayer for Comfort
Committal
Benediction

A graveside service would be structured to be brief:

Call to Worship
Old Testament Reading
The Lord's Prayer
New Testament Reading
Brief Sermon
Committal
Benediction

## Calls to Worship

"I am the resurrection and the life; he who believes in me, though he die, yet shall he live. (John
11:25)

Come to me, all who labor and are heavy laden,
and I will give you rest. Take my yoke upon you, and
learn from me; for I am gentle and lowly in heart,
and you will find rest for your souls. For my yoke is
easy, and my burden is light. (Matt. 11:28-30)

Trust in the Lord with all thine heart; and lean not unto thine own understanding. In all thy ways acknowledge him, and he shall direct thy paths. (Prov. 3:5-6, KJV)

Have no anxiety about anything, but in everything by prayer and supplication with thanksgiving let your requests be made known to God. And the peace of God, which passes all understanding, will keep your hearts and your minds in Christ Jesus. (Phil. 4:6-7)

## Old Testament Scripture Readings

The Lord is my shepherd; I shall not want. He maketh me to lie down in green pastures: he leadeth me beside the still waters. He restoreth my soul: he leadeth me in the paths of righteousness for his name's sake. Yea, though I walk through the valley of the shadow of death, I will fear no evil; for thou art with me; thy rod and thy staff they comfort me. Thou preparest a table before me in the presence of mine enemies: thou anointest my head with oil; my cup runneth over. Surely goodness and mercy shall follow me all the days of my life: and I will dwell in the house of the Lord for ever. (Ps. 23, KJV)

Bless the Lord, O my soul;
  and all that is within me,
  bless his holy name!
Bless the Lord, O my soul,
  and forget not all his benefits,
who forgives all your iniquity,
  who heals all your diseases,
who redeems your life from the Pit,
  who crowns you with steadfast love and mercy,

who satisfies you with good as long as you live
   so that your youth is renewed like the eagle's.


NO

The Lord works vindication
   and justice for all who are oppressed.
He made known his ways to Moses,
   his acts to the people of Israel.
The Lord is merciful and gracious,
   slow to anger and abounding in steadfast love.
He will not always chide,
   nor will he keep his anger for ever.
He does not deal with us according to our sins,
   nor requite us according to our iniquities.
For as the heavens are high above the earth,
   so great is his steadfast love toward those who fear
      him;
as far as the east is from the west,
   so far does he remove our transgressions from us.
As a father pities his children,
   so the Lord pities those who fear him.
For he knows our frame;
   he remembers that we are dust.


— As for man, his days are like grass;
   he flourishes like a flower of the field;
for the wind passes over it, and it is gone,
   and its place knows it no more.
But the steadfast love of the Lord is from everlasting
     to everlasting
   upon those who fear him,
   and his righteousness to children's children,
to those who keep his covenant
   and remember to do his commandments.
(Ps. 103:1-18)

Listen to me, my people,
  and give ear to me, my nation;
for a law will go forth from me,
  and my justice for a light to the peoples.
My deliverance draws near speedily,
  my salvation has gone forth,
  and my arms will rule the peoples;
the coastlands wait for me,
  and for my arm they hope.
Lift up your eyes to the heavens,
  and look at the earth beneath;
for the heavens will vanish like smoke,
  the earth will wear out like a garment,
  and they who dwell in it will die like gnats;
but my salvation will be for ever,
  and my deliverance will never be ended.
(Isa. 51:4-6)

For the Lord will not
  cast off for ever,
but, though he cause grief, he will have compassion
  according to the abundance of his steadfast love;
for he does not willingly afflict
  or grieve the sons of men.

To crush under foot
  all the prisoners of the earth,
to turn aside the right of a man
  in the presence of the Most High,
to subvert a man in his cause,
  the Lord does not approve.

Who has commanded and it came to pass,
  unless the Lord has ordained it?
Is it not from the mouth of the Most High
  that good and evil come?

Why should a living man complain,
    a man, about the punishment of his sins?

Let us test and examine our ways,
    and return to the Lord!
Let us lift up our hearts and hands
    to God in heaven.
(Lam. 3:31-41)

## Funeral Prayers

Our Father, and our God, we affirm that You are
our Refuge and our Strength, a very present help in
time of trouble. You are the eternal God and You are
our dwelling place. You have promised to be near us
when we call upon You in truth and You offer to us
the assurance that beneath us are the everlasting
arms. We come to You, our Father, as a people who
are hurting, feeling keenly the sting of death and
the loss of a loved one. We would ask, that by the
power of Jesus Christ, who Himself conquered the
grave and death, You would be present with us and
grant to us the comfort, the consolation, the grace,
the love and the peace which You alone can give and
which alone is sufficient for us in this time of our
need. May Your spirit so be with us as we share in
these moments of memorial that we shall fittingly
remember our friend and (brother/sister) and give
glory unto our Lord Jesus Christ, in whose name we
pray. Amen. (From *A Manual for Worship and Service,* 1976, Canadian Baptist)

Almighty God, thou who dost give life to man and
dost receive him again in death, we thank thee for
thy abiding presence and for the grace provided in
Christ Jesus. In our frailty we look to thee for

strength and in our sorrow for comfort. Help us in this hour to put our trust in thee that we may receive light and understanding and a new experience of thy grace unto eternal hope, through Jesus Christ our Lord. Amen. (Franklin M. Segler, *The Broadman Minister's Manual*, 1969, Southern Baptist, p. 46)

Almighty and most merciful God, who hast appointed us to endure sufferings and death with our Lord Jesus Christ before we enter with him into eternal glory: Grant us grace at all times to subject ourselves to thy holy will, and to continue steadfast in the true faith unto the end of our lives; and at all times to find peace and joy in the blessed hope of the resurrection of the dead, and of the glory of the world to come; through the same Jesus Christ our Lord. Amen. (From *Occasional Services*, 1982, Lutheran)

## New Testament Scripture Readings

What shall we then say to these things? If God be for us, who can be against us? He that spared not his own Son, but delivered him up for us all, how shall he not with him also freely give us all things? Who shall lay any thing to the charge of God's elect? It is God that justifieth. Who is he that condemneth? It is Christ that died, yea rather, that is risen again, who is even at the right hand of God, who also maketh intercession for us. Who shall separate us from the love of Christ? shall tribulation, or distress, or persecution, or famine, or nakedness, or peril, or sword? As it is written, For thy sake we are killed all the day long; we are accounted as sheep for the slaughter. Nay, in all these things we are more than conquerers through him that loved us. For I am persuaded, that neither death, nor life, nor angels, nor principalities, nor powers, nor things present, nor things to come, Nor height, nor depth, nor any other creature, shall be able to separate us from the love of God, which is in Christ Jesus our Lord. (Rom. 8:31-39, KJV)

Now this I say, brethren, that flesh and blood cannot inherit the kingdom of God; neither doth corruption inherit incorruption. Behold, I shew you a mystery; We shall not all sleep, but we shall all be changed, In a moment, in the twinkling of an eye, at the last trump: for the trumpet shall sound, and the dead shall be raised incorruptible, and we shall be changed. For this corruptible must put on incorruption, and this mortal must put on immortality. So when this corruptible shall have put on incorruption, and this mortal shall have put on immortality, then shall be brought to pass the saying that is written, Death is swallowed up in victory. O death, where is thy sting? O grave, where is thy victory? The sting of death is sin; and the strength of sin is the law. But thanks be to God, which giveth us the victory through our Lord Jesus Christ. Therefore, my beloved brethren, be ye stedfast, unmoveable, always abounding in the work of the Lord, forasmuch as ye know that your labour is not in vain in the Lord. (1 Cor. 15:50-58, KJV)

Blessed be the God and Father of our Lord Jesus Christ! By his great mercy we have been born anew to a living hope through the resurrection of Jesus Christ from the dead, and to an inheritance which is imperishable, undefiled, and unfading, kept in heaven for you, who by God's power are guarded through faith for a salvation ready to be revealed in the last time. In this you rejoice, though now for a little while you may have to suffer various trials, so that the genuineness of your faith, more precious than gold which though perishable is tested by fire, may redound to praise and glory and honor at the revelation of Jesus Christ. Without having seen him you love him; though you do not now see him you believe in him and rejoice with unutterable and exalted joy. As the outcome of your faith you obtain the salvation of your souls. (1 Pet. 1:3-9)

I heard a loud voice from the throne saying, "Behold, the dwelling of God is with men. He will dwell with them, and they shall be his people, and God himself will be with them; he will wipe away every tear from their eyes, and death shall be no more, neither shall there be mourning nor crying nor pain any more, for the former things have passed away."

And he who sat upon the throne said, "Behold, I make all things new." Also he said, "Write this, for these words are trustworthy and true." And he said to me, "It is done! I am the Alpha and the Omega, the beginning and the end. To the thirsty I will give from the fountain of the water of life without payment. He who conquers shall have this heritage, and I will be his God and he shall be my son. (Rev. 21:3-7)

## The Lord's Model Prayer

*The Lord's Model Prayer may be spoken in unison by those gathered at the graveside.*

Our Father which art in heaven, Hallowed be thy name. Thy kingdom come. Thy will be done in earth, as it is in heaven. Give us this day our daily bread. And forgive us our debts, as we forgive our debtors. And lead us not into temptation, but deliver us from evil: For thine is the kingdom, and the power, and the glory, for ever. Amen. (Matt. 6:9-13, KJV)

## Funeral Poems

### In Heaven

In Heaven,
Some little blades of grass
Stood before God.
"What did you do?"
Then all save one of the little blades
Began eagerly to relate
The merits of their lives.
This one stayed a small way behind,
Ashamed.
Presently, God said,
"And what did you do?"
The little blade answered, "Oh, my Lord.
"Memory is bitter to me,
"For, if I did good deeds,
"I know not of them."
Then God, in all His splendor,
Arose from His throne.
"Oh, best little blade of grass!" He said.
                                    —Stephen Crane


### Prospice

Fear death?—to feel the fog in my throat,
    The mist in my face,
When the snows begin, and the blasts denote
    I am nearing the place,
The power of the night, the press of the storm,
    The post of the foe;
Where he stands, the Arch Fear in a visible form,
    Yet the strong man must go:

For the journey is done and the summit attained,
  And the barriers fall,
Though a battle's to fight ere the guerdon be
    gained,
  The reward of it all.
I was ever a fighter, so—one fight more,
  The best and the last!
I would hate that death bandaged my eyes, and
    forbore,
  And bade me creep past.
No! let me taste the whole of it, fare like my peers
  The heroes of old,
Bear the brunt, in a minute pay glad life's arrears
  Of pain, darkness and cold.
For sudden the worst turns the best to the brave,
  The black minute's at end,
And the elements' rage, the fiend-voices that rave,
  Shall dwindle, shall blend,
Shall change, shall become first a peace out of pain,
  Then a light, then thy breast,
O thou soul of my soul! I shall clasp thee again,
  And with God be the rest!

—Robert Browning


A Psalm of Life

Tell me not, in mournful numbers,
  Life is but an empty dream!—
For the soul is dead that slumbers,
  And things are not what they seem.

Life is real! Life is earnest!
  And the grave is not its goal;
Dust thou art, to dust returnest,
  Was not spoken of the soul.

Not enjoyment, and not sorrow,
  Is our destined end or way;
But to act, that each to-morrow
  Find us farther than to-day.

Art is long, and Time is fleeting,
  And our hearts, though stout and brave,
Still, like muffled drums, are beating
  Funeral marches to the grave.

In the world's broad field of battle,
  In the bivouac of Life,
Be not like dumb, driven cattle!
  Be a hero in the strife!

Trust no Future, howe'er pleasant!
  Let the dead Past bury its dead!
Act,—act in the living Present!
  Heart within, and God o'erhead!

Lives of great men all remind us
  We can make our lives sublime,
And, departing, leave behind us
  Footprints on the sands of time;

Footprints, that perhaps another,
  Sailing o'er life's solemn main,
A forlorn and shipwrecked brother,
  Seeing, shall take heart again.

Let us, then, be up and doing,
  With a heart for any fate;
Still achieving, still pursuing,
  Learn to labor and to wait.
                    —Henry Wadsworth Longfellow

## How Beautiful to Be with God!

How beautiful to be with God,
  When earth is fading like a dream,
And from this mist-encircled shore
  We launch upon the unknown stream!
No doubt, no fear, no anxious care
  But comforted by staff and rod,
In the faith-brightened hour of death
  How beautiful to be with God!
Beyond the partings and the pains,
  Beyond the sighing and the tears,
Oh, beautiful to be with God
  Through all the endless, blessed years—
To see His face, to hear His voice,
  To know Him better day by day,
And love Him as the flowers love light,
  And serve Him as immortals may.
                    —Author Unknown


## Crossing the Bar

Sunset and evening star
  And one clear call for me!
And may there be no moaning of the bar,
  When I put out to sea,

But such a tide as moving seems asleep,
  Too full for sound and foam,
When that which drew from out the boundless deep
  Turns again home.

Twilight and evening bell,
  And after that the dark!
And may there be no sadness of farewell,
  When I embark;

For tho' from out our bourne of Time and Place
  The flood may bear me far,
I hope to see my Pilot face to face
  When I have crost the bar.

—Alfred, Lord Tennyson

from Thanatopsis

So live, that when thy summons comes to join
The innumerable caravan which moves
To that mysterious realm, where each shall take
His chamber in the silent halls of death,
Thou go not, like a quarry-slave at night,
Scourged to his dungeon, but, sustained and
    soothed
By an unfaltering trust, approach thy grave
Like one who wraps the drapery of his couch
About him, and lies down to pleasant dreams.

—William Cullen Bryant

## Scripture Readings for the Graveside

Now if Christ is preached as raised from the dead,
how can some of you say that there is no resurrection
of the dead? But if there is no resurrection of the
dead, then Christ has not been raised; if Christ has
not been raised, then our preaching is in vain and
your faith is in vain. We are even found to be
misrepresenting God, because we testified of God
that he raised Christ, whom he did not raise if it is
true that the dead are not raised. For if the dead are
not raised, then Christ has not been raised. If Christ
has not been raised, your faith is futile and you are
still in your sins. Then those also who have fallen
asleep in Christ have perished. If for this life only we

have hoped in Christ, we are of all men most to be
pitied.

But in fact Christ has been raised from the dead,
the first fruits of those who have fallen asleep. For as
by a man came death, by a man has come also the
resurrection of the dead. For as in Adam all die, so
also in Christ shall all be made alive. But each in his
own order: Christ the first fruits, then at his coming
those who belong to Christ. Then comes the end,
when he delivers the kingdom to God the Father
after destroying every rule and every authority and
power. For he must reign until he has put all his
enemies under his feet. The last enemy to be de-
stroyed is death. (1 Cor. 15:12-26)


Verily, verily, I say unto you, He that heareth my
word, and believeth on him that sent me, hath
everlasting life, and shall not come into condemna-
tion; but is passed from death unto life. Verily, verily,
I say unto you, The hour is coming, and now is, when
the dead shall hear the voice of the Son of God: and
they that hear shall live. For as the Father hath life
in himself; so hath he given to the Son to have life in
himself; And hath given him authority to execute
judgment also, because he is the Son of man. Marvel
not at this: for the hour is coming, in the which all
that are in the graves shall hear his voice, And shall
come forth; they that have done good, unto the
resurrection of life; and they that have done evil,
unto the resurrection of damnation. (John 5:24-29,
KJV)


For this reason I bow my knees before the Father,
from whom every family in heaven and on earth is

named, that according to the riches of his glory he may grant you to be strengthened with might through his Spirit in the inner man, and that Christ may dwell in your hearts through faith; that you, being rooted and grounded in love, may have power to comprehend with all the saints what is the breadth and length and height and depth, and to know the love of Christ which surpasses knowledge, that you may be filled with all the fulness of God.

Now to him who by the power at work within us is able to do far more abundantly than all that we ask or think, to him be glory in the church and in Christ Jesus to all generations, for ever and ever. Amen. (Eph. 3:14-21)

*At the death of a Christian, the following may be read:*

Let not your heart be troubled: ye believe in God, believe also in me. In my Father's house are many mansions: if it were not so, I would have told you. I go to prepare a place for you. And if I go and prepare a place for you, I will come again, and receive you unto myself; that where I am, there ye may be also. And whither I go ye know, and the way ye know. Thomas saith unto him, Lord, we know not whither thou goest; and how can we know the way? Jesus saith unto him, I am the way, the truth, and the life: no man cometh unto the Father, but by me. (John 14:1-6, KJV)

## Committal of the Body

*A visible activity, such as the sprinkling of dirt on the coffin, may accompany the words of committal.*

Forasmuch as it hath pleased Almighty God of his great mercy, to take unto himself the soul of our brother: we therefore commit his body to the ground; earth to earth, ashes to ashes, dust to dust; in sure and certain hope of the resurrection to eternal life through our Lord Jesus Christ; who shall change the body of our low estate, that it may be fashioned like unto his glorious body, according to the working whereby he is able even to subdue all things unto himself. (From *Occasional Services,* 1982, Lutheran)

*In the death of a Christian,*

Forasmuch as almighty God hath received unto himself the soul of our departed brother, we therefore tenderly commit his body to the ground, in the blessed hope that as he hath borne the image of the earthly so also he shall bear the image of the heavenly. (From *The Book of Worship,* 1964, Methodist)

*A doxology may be used.*

O the depth of the riches and wisdom and knowledge of God! How unsearchable are his judgments and how inscrutable his ways!
"For who has known the mind of the Lord,
    or who has been his counselor?"
"Or who has given a gift to him that he might be
    repaid?"
For from him and through him and to him are all things. To him be glory for ever. Amen. (Rom. 11:33-36)

## Benedictions

Now may the God of peace who brought again
from the dead our Lord Jesus, the great shepherd of
the sheep, by the blood of the eternal covenant, equip
you with everything good that you may do his will,
working in you that which is pleasing in his sight,
through Jesus Christ; to whom be glory for ever and
ever. Amen. (Heb. 13:20-21)

Blessed be the God and Father of our Lord Jesus
Christ! By his great mercy we have been born anew
to a living hope through the resurrection of Jesus
Christ from the dead, and to an inheritance which is
imperishable, undefiled, and unfading, kept in
heaven for you. (1 Pet. 1:3-4)

For I am sure that neither death, nor life, nor
angels, nor principalities, nor things present, nor
things to come, nor powers, nor height, nor depth,
nor anything else in all creation, will be able to
separate us from the love of God in Christ Jesus our
Lord. (Rom. 8:38-39)

Now to him who is able to keep you from falling
and to present you without blemish before the presence of his glory with rejoicing, to the only God, our
Savior through Jesus Christ our Lord, be glory,
majesty, dominion, and authority, before all time
and now and for ever. Amen. (Jude 24-25)

"And, now let God's gentle earth blanket the form
of this, His child, in calm and peace, who is now of
worldly cares divest, and in quiet repose will await
the final dawn." (Mrs. Rebecca Todd Tribble)

# 6
# The Parent-Child Dedication Service

The parent-child dedication service is a relatively recent phenomenon which is practiced in those churches which do not baptize their children as infants. Having rejected the idea that parents can claim the kingdom of God for their children, many evangelical churches have nonetheless recognized the vast importance of a rite of passage for both children and parents after a child's birth. This rite of passage allows that God is at work, as are the parents, on behalf of the child, even this early in life, to bring him or her into the Lord's kingdom.

This worship emphasis prevents the child from being in a kind of spiritual "no-man's-land" from birth until that unspecified time that evangelicals call the "age of accountability." A parent-child dedication service provides an occasion in which responsibilities are announced and accepted by the parents themselves (therefore, a parent dedication), and in which, until the child is able to choose for himself or herself, God is asked to reign over the life of the child (therefore, a child dedication).

Simultaneously, the church should be asked to dedicate itself to the task of nurturing and sustaining the child. Especially in an era when extended families are small and scattered, youngsters need adult friends and Christian models as they grow to maturity.

A parent-child dedication service does not ensure a child safe passage into heaven. Certainly, the act of dedicating a child to God, combined with the act of the parents dedicating themselves to God, increases that child's "chances" of making a mature decision to let Christ be Lord of his or her life. But the service does not "save" the child, either for the short term (until maturity) or for the long term (through eternity). For the former, we count on God's grace. For the latter, along with God's grace, we trust the child to make his or her own decision of faith.

This needs to be stressed, because some misunderstanding exists at this point. Sometimes, the problem is a result of modern ecumenicity in which well-intentioned but misinformed Christians from infant-baptizing congregations believe that your church holds to the same theology as their home church. Other times, the problem is purely pagan, with parents thinking that the service will somehow magically ensure their child's eternal security. One of my most frustrating experiences as a pastor was one of my first parent-child dedication services. I was late in announcing the service to my congregation, so the ill-planned service was open to whichever parents and children "showed up." One mother, daughter, and grandmother came, whom I had never seen before, whose names I did not learn in the rush before the worship service, and whom I have never seen since. The husband, if there was one, stayed home. I sincerely hope that mom and grandmom did not expect their infant to enter the kingdom of God based on what took place that Sunday morning. But I suspect that is exactly what they thought. Since then, both my preparation and my homily have attempted to clarify any confusion in this regard.

Age does not make a difference in the child being dedicated, unless he or she is obviously past the age of ability to make his or her own decision to trust the Lord. Then, the youngster should be encouraged to make his or her own choice. This allowance for age variance permits adults who are new Christians, or parents who have previously worshiped in a church which did not have such a service, to dedicate each of their children. It would border on the withholding of a blessing to participate in a parent-child dedication service with a two-month-old child and leave out the four- and five-year-old children of the same couple, if they have never been through such an experience with their parents.

## Planning a Parent-Child Dedication Service

The parent-child dedication service should be built around those Scripture passages which give us a theology of children and a theology of parenting. Response is an important part of this service, as the parents and the church commit themselves to their respective covenants.

Both the parents and the child(ren) should be introduced. Every effort should be made to keep the service of worship personal for each of those involved, whatever their total number might be.

If the parents leave the sanctuary to return their children to the church's nursery (and they usually do) after the charges and dedications, then it is important for them to understand that they are to return to the sanctuary for the remainder of the service. The sermon, hymns, and the remainder of the liturgy will have been structured with them in mind. This should go without saying, but excited moms and dads might need a reminder so they don't stay in the nursery with their children for the entire service.

Parent-child dedication services should be scheduled as often as necessary to make the event meaningful for those persons involved. An assembly line atmosphere with too many children and parents can make the event less meaningful. Schedule more than one dedication service a year if necessary. Also, the "rut" of holding parent-child dedication services only on Mother's Day needs to be broken. Alternate between Mother's Day and Father's Day every year or schedule this worship service on Children's Day or a "neutral" Sunday. The father's responsibility in parenting, which is too often ignored, needs emphasis, not disregard.

An appropriate order of worship might be structured as follows:

Prelude
Call to Worship
Invocation
Hymn about the Family
Old Testament Scripture
Introduction of Parents and Children
Parent-Child-Church Covenant
Dedicatory Prayer
Choral Response/Amen
Hymn of Praise
Offertory Prayer
Organ Meditation
Choral Anthem
New Testament Scripture
Sermon
Hymn of Commitment
Benediction
Postlude

## Calls to Worship

Train up a child in the way he should go,
    and when he is old he will not depart from it.
(Prov. 22:6)


The steadfast love of the Lord is from everlasting to
        everlasting
    upon those who fear him,
    and his righteousness to children's children,
to those who keep his covenant
    and remember to do his commandments.
(Ps. 103:17-18)

Let the children come to me, do not hinder them; for to such belongs the kingdom of God. (Mark 10:14)

Come, ye children, hearken unto me: I will teach you the fear of the Lord. (Ps. 34:11, KJV)

To all who received him, who believed in his name, he gave power to become children of God. (John 1:12)

## Parent-Child-Church Covenants

PASTOR: Do you promise to so conduct your own lives that your children may learn of the Lord Jesus Christ by your example?
PARENTS: We do.
PASTOR: Do you promise to pray for your children daily?
PARENTS: We do.
PASTOR: Do you promise to instruct your children in the ways of the Lord, to teach them his Word, and to talk with them about faith in Jesus as Savior and Lord when they reach an age of spiritual understanding?
PARENTS: We do.
PASTOR: As a congregation, you have heard the promises of these parents. But they will be unable to achieve all their hopes and dreams for the enrichment of their children alone. Bringing up children is a community effort. For them to grow up to be all that they might be spiritually, emotionally, and physically, we will all have to help. We need to be a kind of extended family for these children. Do you, as a congregation, promise to support the efforts of these parents with your prayers, and your words and acts of encouragement?
CONGREGATION: We do.

PASTOR: Having heard the promises of both these parents and the gathered church, I commend both them and their children to the care of God and to his immeasurable grace.

LEADER: Do you recognize your responsibility as parents and do you bring your child here in dedication to God in the presence of this church as a sign of your dependence on divine help to fulfill your parental duties?

PARENTS: We do.

LEADER: Do you solemnly commit yourselves to seek to bring up your child in the nurture and knowledge of God?

PARENTS: We do.

LEADER: Do you commit yourselves to use all the resources available to teach and lead your child both to experience a personal relationship with Christ and to develop a Christlike character?

PARENTS: We do.

LEADER: Do you faithfully commit yourselves to try to provide the home life and the church experience that will shape the kind of environment that will enable your child to profess Christ as Lord and serve him as Master?

PARENTS: We do.

LEADER: If you, the church, realize your responsibility to help in providing the kind of environment that will point children to Christ and help them to grow in the life God intends, will you rise? Do you commit yourselves to seek to fulfill your responsibility?

PEOPLE: We do.

(From Robert Bailey, *New Ways in Christian Wor-*

*ship* [Nashville: Broadman Press, 1981], pp. 121-122.)

MINISTER: Do you, parents, desire earnestly that your child shall grow up in the "nurture and admonition of the Lord"?
PARENTS: We do.
MINISTER: Do you covenant together to strive to bring to him a knowledge of the Scriptures, to teach him loving, obedient reverence for God and for his Son, Jesus Christ, and to use all the agencies of the church to accomplish this end?
PARENTS: We do.
MINISTER: As you dedicate this child today, do you also desire to dedicate yourselves, as parents, to Christ and the church, that you may live exemplary lives and so living may present and commend Christ to your child from his youth up?
PARENTS: We do.
MINISTER: Having heard these vows and sacred promises I, as your minister, do solemnly and joyfully commend this child to the divine care and protection of God, our heavenly Father, for all the years of his life. (American Baptist, Judson Press © 1969)

PASTOR: "Let the children come to me, and do not hinder them; for to such belongs the kingdom of God." (Luke 18:16)
CONGREGATION: "Truly, I say to you, whoever does not receive the kingdom of God like a child shall not enter it." (Luke 18:17)
PASTOR: Do not provoke your children to anger, but bring them up in the discipline and instruction of the Lord. (Eph. 6:4)

PARENTS: We will teach our children to trust the Lord.

PASTOR: Trust in the Lord with all thine heart; and lean not unto thine own understanding. In all thy ways acknowledge him, and he shall direct thy paths. (Prov. 3:5-6, KJV)

PARENTS: We will trust the Lord.

## Dedicatory Prayers

Dear Lord Jesus, Lover of children, look down on these little ones and their parents with your divine favor. Grant them your wisdom, your compassion, and a human spirit that is in the image of your Holy Spirit, through Jesus Christ our Lord. Amen.

Our Father, whose home is in heaven, we pray now for the earthly home of these little children. Most important, we ask that as they grow older, that they turn to you as Savior and Lord. We pray that they grow in their understanding of your will for them during their days among us. We pray for friends for them that would please you. We pray for the husbands and wives that these youngsters will someday marry. May they choose their life's partner wisely, looking to you for guidance. We pray for the measure of health that we all want our children to enjoy. We pray for the personalities of these innocent and unspoiled children. We want them to be fun to be around, helpful in their efforts, sincere in their commitments, and disciplined in their responsibilities. We want these children to have hobbies and interests, an education, and a vocation that fits their skills and that pleases you. We ask for a lot for these children, Lord, not just because they belong to us, but because they also belong to you. So we pray, certain of your loving response, in the name of Jesus. Amen.

O God of all time and of every age, O Father of all humankind and of every person, O Spirit in the limitless space and in us, We praise you for who you are and for what you are trying to make of us. You are worthy of all praise. We praise you for childhood: the wonder of dripping faucets, finding peculiar shaped rocks, touching worms as they measure the sidewalk, birds singing in the morning, sounds of night after we go to bed, throwing rocks in the lake, picking wild flowers, ice-cream cones dripping on our chins, riding on Dad's shoulders, listening to Mother read a story, learning to ride a bicycle with training wheels, then without, being able to cry when we are hurt, being able to laugh when something is funny. We praise you for youthhood: an expanding world of people and places, growing taller and developing, becoming coordinated at last, the noise of a transistor, the quiet strings as they play a folk song, uncritical friends who accept us, teachers who equip us to function in our world, parents who understand us, places to hang out, the touch of a friend's hand, discipline of the arts and of sports. We praise you for adulthood: seeing the shades of blue on deep waters dashed with sparkles from the sun, hues of green on the tiered hills of eastern Kentucky, the embrace of a faithful marriage mate, the satisfaction of hard work, the responsibility for providing a home, a church, and the institutions of society, hearing the uninhibited laughter of children splashing in a swimming pool, participating in the maturing of energetic teenagers around us, friends who are glad to see us. Yes, O God, we praise you for this life; and though there are times when there is no song on our lips because there is no joy in our hearts, we thank you for those joys that make us want to sing every song we hear. Amen. (G. Temp Sparkman)

Creator God, for the beauty and the wonder of birth and new life, we give our thanks. At no time is your majesty more apparent than when we see your creation. And in your wisdom, you have let men and women be a part of your creative process. But instead of feeling powerful, we feel humbled. We know that life is no mere accident, no haphazard event. So we praise you!

Ever-present Creator, we need to be reminded that you do not stop making us and molding us at our physical birth. Instead, as long as we let you, you shape us into a son or a daughter who is pleasing to you. May our renewed sense of awe in the presence of your handiwork today be sustained as we move from this exciting day to the routines of life.

Compassionate Lord, we worship you because you are our hope and our source of strength at all times. From birth to the grave, you are our sure and certain Helper. Let this day be a time of renewal in each of our lives. Amen.

## Benedictions

Now may our Lord Jesus Christ himself, and God our Father, who loved us and gave us eternal comfort and good hope through grace, comfort your hearts and establish them in every good work and word. (2 Thess. 2:16-17)

Be subject to one another out of reverence for Christ. (Eph. 5:21)

Guard the truth that has been entrusted to you by the Holy Spirit who dwells within us. (2 Tim. 1:14)

Fare ye well in God the Father, and in Jesus Christ, our common hope. Amen. (Ignatius)

# 7
# Other Dedication or Installation Services

Anything that can be set apart for religious purposes may be dedicated or installed in a worship setting.

The most common dedication ceremony is the "blessing" or "grace" that is said before meals in many Christian (and, for that matter, non-Christian) homes. A typical prayer of blessing asks God to use the food that is about to be eaten to nourish the body *in order that God might be better served*.

In an insightful little essay about prayer, Eliot Carey asks the question, "How much prayer should a hamburger get?"[1] He asks if a prayer at grocery-buying time would eliminate the need for all of the individual prayers at each meal. He is asking a question about our dedication of various resources, gifts, and material possessions.

My answer to his question: "We need more opportunities for dedication, not fewer!" The hamburger has not been prayed over too much if a prayer is offered to God at both the time of its purchase and at the time of its consumption. Of course, we're really not praying so much for the hamburger as we are for ourselves, that we will be good stewards of our resources and that God will sustain us with daily bread (and in the case of hamburger, meat).

All of this is to say that it is hard to overpray. Thus, anything which can be set apart for religious purposes may be dedicated or installed in a worship setting.

Churches have installed Sunday School teachers and church officers; they have commissioned choirs, and other groups and individuals for special service (for example, a short-term mission project); and they have dedicated church buildings, homes, denominational buildings (for example, hospitals, conference centers, and college dormitories), organs, hymn books, stained glass windows, pew cushions, flags, and ice makers for the fellowship hall.

If God can use something, then it is worth the time and trouble required to ask him to be the primary agent in its proper use. But the prayer aspect is only one facet of a dedication. The other directly involves the church in its commitment to a covenant relationship regarding the subject at hand.

A dedication service should include some commitments by the person or congregation making the dedicatory effort. The relationship is not just one way, asking God to do his part. We commit ourselves to some responsibilities.

For an example, consider the termination of a church's relationship with its building. A congregation grows large and needs to move to another tract of land. The old building must be sold. Many economic and legal matters get involved, but the primary consideration should still be spiritual. If the building was dedicated to the glory of God at its erection, and it should have been, then I question whether a church should sell out to the highest bidder, regardless of who that bidder is. I would rather see the building sold to a smaller church of another denomination, or turned into a community library, than to be sold to a nightclub chain whose activities will not glorify God.

The Bible records several instances of dedication services. Numbers 7:10 tells of the dedication of the altar of the tabernacle, while 2 Chronicles 7:9 describes the dedication of the altar in Solomon's Temple. Nehemiah 12:27 gives an account of the dedication of the rebuilt wall of Jerusalem. The most thorough account of a dedication ceremony is 1 Kings 8, describing the events surrounding the dedication of Solomon's Temple. Though most evangelical churches would not be receptive to passages from the Apocrypha being used as the primary text for a worship service, the account of the rededication of the Temple found in 1 Maccabees 4:36-61 is a moving story which could amplify or illustrate a dedication service.

"Utensils" are sanctified or set apart for special use by God in 2 Chronicles 29:19, indicating that nothing is too small or insignificant to be bypassed in the dedicatory process.

The same worship elements are seen in the biblical accounts of dedication that we find in other kinds of worship: intercessory prayers, doxologies, didactic and kerygmatic lessons. Indeed, in the New Testament the kerygmatic message would replace the sacrifices so common in the Old Testament dedicatory ceremonies. Sacrifices of twenty-two thousand oxen and one hundred and twenty thousand sheep (Solomon's offering at the Temple dedication, 1 Kings 8:62-63) are redundant in the context of the New Testament Church. The crucifixion of Jesus ends any sacrificial responsibility which might be required for pleasing God. He is most pleased with a simple confession of our faith.

## Planning a Dedication or Installation Service

An entire worship service is *not* necessary in order to dedicate, sanctify, or set apart something or someone for God's use. As with the hamburger, Sunday School teachers may be prayed for not only at a once-a-year installation service but also on a weekly basis during the church's regular worship period. The piano and the record player may be used as a constant reminder to kids in a children's choir group that God provides for us in many ways and that we respond to him in just as many different ways.

For the "utensils" of a church, a briefer time of dedication might be most appropriate, and the proper setting may be something other than a normal Lord's Day worship service. A churchwide fellowship meal would probably be the best time to dedicate the new ice maker. The Sunday School class would be the best setting in which to dedicate the new couch, chairs, coffee pot, and end tables that will make for a more relaxed learning environment.

To devote an entire service to a dedication of the new pew cushions or the new carpet could give a disproportionate emphasis to material comforts which really are optional in God's work. But to ignore God's ability to use even these mundane items is to miss an opportunity to be involved with God and with one another in a covenant relationship which has dimensions in all parts of our lives.

On the other hand, it is hard to imagine the setting aside for spiritual purposes of something which involves obviously large expenditures of resources or some person or persons without a major worship emphasis to dedicate the object or person.

In reading 1 Kings 8, several lessons may be learned. First, those involved in the dedication are those to whom the event has the most meaning. Solomon assembled the elders and leaders of Israel, as well as all the men (people?). Though it may not hurt to have mayors and legislators present, and though ministers from other local churches might be interested, it is right for the people within the local church who are most vitally involved with the project (whatever it may be) to be the most prominently incorporated into the procedures of the day (whatever they may be).[2]

Second, leave room for God's involvement. Don't schedule him out of the process. I am impressed that in verse 10 of 1 Kings 8, the cloud which represented the glory of the Lord so filled the Temple that the priests had to come out of the holy place. Sometimes, when our ceremonial footwork gets too fancy, I think that we reverse the event, and we run God out of his house. Leave room for God to act and be involved.

Third, recognize the limits of our human efforts. Solomon, in his prayer (v. 27), asked the legitimate question, "Will God indeed dwell on the earth?" Would God reside in a house built with human hands when the highest heaven was unable to contain the Lord? For all of our dedications, a similar question is necessary. Can God use these hymnbooks when all of the words of all humankind cannot adequately express our praises? To our God who has given us the task of going into all of the world, is our new church bus that very significant? Surely, we are humbled by such thoughts, as was Solomon, but we boldly approach God's throne of grace and petition him for favor.

Fourth, we unashamedly make reference to and emphasize the thing or person which we are dedicating. In Solomon's prayer in 1 Kings 8, he makes reference to "this house," "this place," which he has built and which is being dedicated no less than eight times. You really don't appreciate the logic and order of his lengthy prayer until you read it in a Bible where the verses are grouped in paragraphs. If something is worth setting apart for God's purposes and use, then we need not be embarrassed by it. Enjoy it, and talk with God and with one another about it with forthrightness and assurance. He will honor his covenant relationships. We are reminded of this in the benediction found in verses 56-58.

Fifth, the dedication of Solomon's Temple was a time of joy and festivity. A week-long celebration was associated with it. The Jewish holiday Hanukkah is a result of the establishment of the Feast of Dedication, when the Maccabees reconsecrated the Temple in Jerusalem. Probably, we are a little too stern-faced in our dedications, reading serious litanies, importing denominational executives, and generally acting pompous. The Temple dedications of Solomon and the Maccabees are reminders that we should use these events as opportunities for celebration.

The dedication service for a new building might be structured in the following manner:

Prelude
Doxology
Invocation
Hymn of Praise
Welcome and Introduction of Guests
   1. Architect
   2. General Contractor
   3. Denominational Workers
   4. Other
Choral Anthem
New Testament Scripture
Prayer of Dedication
Charges
   1. Chairperson of the Building Committee
   2. Chairperson of the Deacons
   3. Pastor
Hymn of Dedication
Old Testament Scripture
Fellowship Period/Meal
Benediction

The dedication of a relatively minor article for sacred use might consist of little more than Scripture and a prayer:
Scripture
Statement of Purpose/Charge
Silent Prayer
Dedicatory Prayer by Pastor/Teacher/Group Leader
Doxology (Spoken in Unison)

## Calls to Worship

Thus says the Lord: "Let not the wise man glory in his wisdom, let not the mighty man glory in his might, let not the rich man glory in his riches; but

let him who glories glory in this, that he under-
stands and knows me, that I am the Lord who
practices steadfast love, justice, and righteousness in
the earth; for in these things I delight, says the
Lord." (Jer. 9:23-24)

The earth is the Lord's, and the fulness thereof;
the world, and they that dwell therein. (Ps. 24:1,
KJV)

*For any dedication that has to do with the music,*

I will give thanks to the Lord with my whole heart;
    I will tell of all thy wonderful deeds.
I will be glad and exult in thee,
    I will sing praise to thy name, O Most High.
(Ps. 9:1-2)

*For any dedication that has to do with buildings,*

Enlarge the place of your tent,
    and let the curtains of your habitations be
        stretched out;
hold not back, lengthen your cords
    and strengthen your stakes.
For you will spread abroad to the right and to the
        left,
    and your descendants will possess the nations
    and will people the desolate cities.
(Isa. 54:2-3)

## Old Testament Scripture Readings

The rest of the people, the priests, the Levites, the
gatekeepers, the singers, the temple servants, and
all who have separated themselves from the peoples

of the lands to the law of God, their wives, their sons, their daughters, all who have knowledge and understanding, join with their brethren, their nobles, and enter into a curse and an oath to walk in God's law which was given by Moses the servant of God, and to observe and do all the commandments of the Lord our Lord and his ordinances and his statutes. (Neh. 10:28-29)

Then Solomon assembled the elders of Israel and all the heads of the tribes, the leaders of the fathers' houses of the people of Israel, before King Solomon in Jerusalem, to bring up the ark of the covenant of the Lord out of the city of David, which is Zion. And all the men of Israel assembled to King Solomon at the feast in the month Ethanim, which is the seventh month. And all the elders of Israel came, and the priests took up the ark. And they brought up the ark of the Lord, the tent of meeting, and all the holy vessels that were in the tent; the priests and the Levites brought them up. And King Solomon and all the congregation of Israel, who had assembled before him, were with him before the ark, sacrificing so many sheep and oxen that they could not be counted or numbered. Then the priests brought the ark of the covenant of the Lord to its place, in the inner sanctuary of the house, in the most holy place, underneath the wings of the cherubim. (1 Kings 8:1-6)

All the utensils which King Ahaz discarded in his reign when he was faithless, we have made ready and sanctified; and behold, they are before the altar of the Lord. (2 Chron. 29:19)

How lovely is thy dwelling place,
    O Lord of hosts!
My soul longs, yea, faints
    for the courts of the Lord;
my heart and flesh sing for joy to the living God.

Even the sparrow finds a home,
    and the swallow a nest for herself,
    where she may lay her young,
at thy altars, O Lord of hosts,
    my King and my God.
Blessed are those who dwell in thy house,
    ever singing thy praise!
(Ps. 84:1-4)

## New Testament Scripture Readings

For we are God's fellow workers; you are God's
field, God's building.

According to the grace of God given to me, like a
skilled master builder I laid a foundation, and
another man is building upon it. Let each man take
care how he builds upon it. For no other foundation
can any one lay than that which is laid, which is
Jesus Christ. Now if any one builds on the foundation with gold, silver, precious stones, wood, hay,
straw—each man's work will become manifest; for
the Day will disclose it, because it will be revealed
with fire, and the fire will test what sort of work each
one has done. If the work which any man has built
on the foundation survives, he will receive a reward.
(1 Cor. 3:9-14)

Come to him, to that living stone, rejected by men
but in God's sight chosen and precious; and like
living stones be yourselves built into a spiritual

house, to be a holy priesthood, to offer spiritual
sacrifices acceptable to God through Jesus Christ.
For it stands in scripture:
"Behold, I am laying in Zion a stone,
   a cornerstone chosen and precious,
and he who believes in him will not be put to
   shame."
(1 Pet. 2:4-6)

*For commissioning services,*

It shall not be so among you; but whoever would be
great among you must be your servant, and whoever
would be first among you must be your slave; even as
the Son of man came not to be served but to serve,
and to give his life as a ransom for many." (Matt.
20:26-28)

And his gifts were that some should be apostles,
some prophets, some evangelists, some pastors and
teachers, to equip the saints for the work of ministry,
for building up the body of Christ until we all attain
to the unity of the faith and of the knowledge of the
Son of God, to mature manhood, to the measure of
the stature of the fulness of Christ. (Eph. 4:11-13)

## Dedicatory Prayers

Lord, we offer this _____ (object) to you for your
use. We are humbled to think that you would take
our efforts and make them significant in your kingdom's work. We offer but little to you compared to
what you have given us; but in your grace, you accept
our gifts and multiply our efforts. For all of your
gifts, we give you our thanks. Now, Lord, help us to
be good stewards of that which you have entrusted to

us. Help us to use our own and our church's material blessings to accomplish your kingdom's purposes. We pray in the name and for the sake of our Lord Jesus. Amen.

*For installation of church leaders,*

Kind and gracious Heavenly Father, that you would work in partnership with us continues to be one of the great mysteries of creation. Yet, you do ask us to participate in the great drama of the reconciliation and the redemption of the world.

Today, Father, we set aside _____ (person or persons) for service to your kingdom's work. May you empower them with your Holy Spirit. May you enrich them with your love. May you energize them with your hope, that your children have a sure and certain reward when we serve you.

Dear Father, we ask for your blessings upon these your children. May their spiritual roots grow deep as they follow you. Through your Son Jesus, we pray. Amen.

## Doxologies

To the King of Ages, immortal, invisible, the only God, be honor and glory for ever and ever. Amen. (1 Tim. 1:17)

Blessed be the Lord, the God of my master Abraham, who has not forsaken his steadfast love and his faithfulness. (Gen. 24:27)

Now to him who by the power at work within us is able to do far more abundantly than all that we ask or think, to him be glory in the church and in Christ

Jesus to all generations, for ever and ever. Amen.
(Eph. 3:20-21)

## Benedictions

Create in me a clean heart, O God,
  and put a new and right spirit within me.
Cast me not away from thy presence,
  and take not thy holy Spirit from me.
Restore to me the joy of thy salvation,
  and uphold me with a willing spirit.
(Ps. 51:10-12)

May the Lord direct your hearts to the love of God
and to the steadfastness of Christ. (2 Thess. 3:5)

And now I commend you to God and to the word of
his grace, which is able to build you up and to give
you the inheritance among all those who are sanctified. (Acts 20:32)

"The Lord watch between you and me, when we
are absent one from the other." (Gen. 31:49)

### Notes

1. Eliot Carey, *"How Much Prayer Should a Hamburger
Get?"*, comp. William J. Krutza (Grand Rapids: Baker Book
House, 1975), pp. 42-48.
2. The worship element at the conclusion of this chapter allows
for the introduction of "distinguished guests" but does not
encourage speeches by these persons or any other kind of
significant worship involvement on their part.

# 8
# The Ordination Service

Christians should have a "high" theology of baptism and a relatively "low" theology of ordination. Christians seriously believe in the idea of a conventional community. They have a right to expect that all persons in that fellowship, both laity and clergy, will invest themselves fully for the good of the kingdom of God. Certainly any kind of behavioral double standard is wrong. If swearing is bad, then it is bad for every Christian. If peacemaking pleases Jesus, then every Christian should be involved in this venture. If offering salvation (preaching) can be done by one Christian, it can be done by all. If one Christian might baptize a new believer, then so might any other Christian do the same, with the church's authorization.

Dean Kelly has observed a distinct correlation between the seriousness with which churches treat membership in their organization and their prosperity for growth. He calls it the "power of the gate." Churches that let just anybody become a part of their membership, who will baptize anyone who asks, have a slower growth rate than those churches who require certain evidences of Christian repentance from those who are baptized into their membership. Both their theology and practice indicate that these latter churches have a "high" theology of baptism.

But must there necessarily be a "lowering" of their theology of ordination? Yes. The Christian faith radically differs from its Jewish heritage in its concept of the priesthood. Where Old Testament Judaism conceived of their priests as the go-between for God and his people, New Testament Christianity is very specific that there is only one mediator between God and man, one high priest, Christ Jesus (1 Tim. 2:5, Heb. 4:14-16; 8:1-2). Instead of a hierarchy of superspiritual priests with privileged access to God, all Christians are part of a royal and holy priesthood (1 Pet. 2:5,9).

Given that background, it is a wonder that Christianity ever developed a "professional clergy." But it did, and that was probably as much the result of practical considerations as anything else. Men and women who are gifted and skilled in certain areas should be, as a matter of good stewardship, given the opportunity to use those gifts and skills as much as possible. Normal functional offices in the early New Testament churches included, for example, both traveling prophets and prophetesses and local, stationary overseers (bishops) or elders. In addition, young men and women, still uncertain of the extent of their gifts or skills, might have been set apart or consecrated for a certain missionary task as representatives of their church.

Since anything or anyone can be set apart for special use by God and for his kingdom's work (see chapter 7), then ordination becomes either a substitution for or an extension of that concept. It is a substitution in that ordination is really no more than a recognition or commissioning service of a pastor, deacon, missionary, or denominational servant. It is an extension in that ordination supplements the biblical teachings on other, general dedications. Had not the New Testament actually used the word *ordain* (which it does in such places as Titus 1:5 and 1 Timothy 2:7), then the twentieth century church might have adapted just as well with such words as *consecrate, commission,* or *dedicate*.

Since we do have the word, however, it has taken on its own specialized usage. Always having to do with people and not things, ordination is usually reserved for initiation into the pastoral ministry.[1]

Any Scripture which has to do with relationships between the professional clergy and the laity (such as the entire Book of Malachi) or between the religious leadership and the "common people" (for example, Jesus' admonitions to the scribes and Pharisees) might have bearing on our attitudes and Christian understandings about ordination. The question is not whether certain individuals will be set apart at certain times in the life of the church for certain tasks, but the question instead is, "How set apart will they be?"

Two passages of Scripture dominate our thinking about ordination. In the Old Testament, Leviticus, chapters 8 and 9, is a description of the ordination of Aaron and his sons by Moses. Most of the narrative is concerned with sacrificial details which do not directly concern the Christian church except as they remind us of the overwhelming grace of God that allows us the privilege of both being and serving in his kingdom.

Still, those two chapters are brimful of advice to us about ordination procedures. As with other kinds of significant dedications, the congregation is assembled. As helpful as it is to have other pastors present, especially those who were involved in the ordination council, do not schedule an afternoon service if the majority of the congregation of the ordinand will not attend.

The "calling" of a pastor into the ministry and the ordination of that pastor generally involves too few people anyway. The normal pattern is that a person "feels called," shares with the pastor, finds an opportunity for ministry, goes before an examining council, and then is ordained. In most cases, the actual ordination service is the only place that the entire congregation gets involved. Don't lessen what little involvement the congregation already has.

In verse 6 of chapter 8, Aaron and his sons were washed with water and cleansed. The Christian parallels of this act would be baptism and confession. Since every candidate for ordination would have been baptized into the church already, a time of confession, of cleansing from sin immediately before the actual ordination, would be appropriate.

In verse 8 of the same chapter, Moses gives Aaron the Urim and Thummim. Bible scholars have not been able to determine exactly what these objects were, but we do know that they were objects used to determine God's will. (See Num. 27:21.) Such ancient practice is excellent precedent for the modern-day practice of giving the ordinand a Bible as part of the ordination ceremony. The Bible is the primary tool used by the New Testament pastor to determine God's will.

Verse 33 tells us that the ordination of Aaron was a seven-day process. Though I don't believe that the length needs to be mimicked in exact detail, I do think the length of that first biblical ordination should remind us that this is not to be a hasty event. Too frequently, ordination services have already been scheduled to take place immediately following the examining council's meeting. Such presetting of the ordination service tends to make a mockery out of the examination council's efforts. Sufficient time should be allowed throughout the process: from the time of the initial call to the organization of an examination council to the actual ordination.

The end of chapter 9 of Leviticus concludes the two-week event during which Aaron was ordained. Aaron himself gives the benediction. Again, this practice has survived until today, when it is common for the ordinand to pronounce the benediction at the close of the ordination service.

The major New Testament passage which influences our ordination practices is Acts 13:1-3. In this Scripture, a council of prophets and teachers is led by the Holy Spirit to commend Barnabas and Saul for missionary work. After fasting and prayer, they "lay their hands" on these two men, and send them off to their task.

Here we have the model for the ordination councils of the New Testament church. God's initiative is stressed. A practice is commended, involving the "laying on of hands," whose antecedents are in the anointings of the Old Testament. Moses anointed Aaron in Leviticus 8:12. This anointing foreshadows the practice of only ordained persons being involved in the laying on of hands, but this limitation is not a biblical mandate.

Also, we see that Paul and Barnabas were set apart for a specific task. Because of this precedent, it is a rare and unusual circumstance for a person to be ordained without a definite ministry waiting on his or her service and leadership.

Some churches may wish to present the authorization of the examining council for the ordination at some location early in the worship service. This act expresses both the fellowship between sister churches of like faith and practice and the doctrinal soundness of the candidate for ordination. A report of recommendations from both the secretary of the examining council and the church clerk would be appropriate.

A service of ordination might be outlined in the following manner:

Prelude
Call to Worship
Hymn
Old Testament Scripture
Greetings and Authorization
   1. Host Pastor
   2. Examination Council
   3. Church Clerk
Charge to the Candidate

Charge to the Church
Hymn
Ordination Prayer
"Laying on of Hands"
Presentation of the Bible
Benediction of the Ordinand

## Calls to Worship

"This book of the law shall not depart out of your mouth, but you shall meditate on it day and night, that you may be careful to do according to all that is written in it; for then you shall make your way prosperous, and then you shall have good success. Have I not commanded you? Be strong and of good courage; be not frightened, neither be dismayed; for the Lord your God is with you wherever you go." (Josh. 1:8-9)

He has showed you, O man, what is good;
  and what does the Lord require of you
but to do justice, and to love kindness,
  and to walk humbly with your God?
(Mic. 6:8)

We know that all things work together for good to them that love God, to them who are the called according to his purpose. (Rom. 8:28, KJV)

Whatsoever ye do in word or deed, do all in the name of the Lord Jesus, giving thanks to God and the Father by him. (Col. 3:17, KJV)

## Ordination Prayers

How simple it is for me to believe in you, O Lord. How easy it is for me to believe.

When I doubt, and my soul is made bare, when even my wisest friends can see no further than I can into the night to know what tomorrow brings, you fill me with the clear certainty that you exist and that you are watching to help me should I stumble in the darkness.

Though you could have led me down a bright and dazzling path through this world, you have let me take a humbler road, so that when others see a light in me, they will know it is your light reflected.

Anything that I reflect originated with you. For that which I will not succeed in reflecting, you will use others. Amen. (Adapted from a prayer by Alexander Solzhenitsyn)

Most Merciful God, our heavenly Father, who through thy beloved Son hast bid us pray for an increase of those who labor in the Gospel: We earnestly beseech thee to bestow thy Holy Spirit upon these thy servants, upon us, and upon all who are called to the Ministry of the Word and the Sacraments. Make us to be numbered in the company of thy true evangelists, and to continue faithful and steadfast against the world, the flesh, and the devil, that in all our words and deeds we may seek thy glory and the increase of thy kingdom; through thy Son, Jesus Christ, our Lord, who liveth and reigneth with thee and the Holy Ghost, one God, world without end. Amen. (From *Occasional Services,* 1982, Lutheran)

Most merciful Father, we beseech thee to send upon these thy servants thy heavenly blessing; that they may be clothed with righteousness, and that thy Word spoken by their mouths may have such success, that it may never be spoken in vain. Grant also, that we may have grace to hear and receive what they shall deliver out of thy most holy Word, or agreeable to the same, as the means of our salvation; that in all our words and deeds we may seek thy glory, and the increase of thy kingdom; through Jesus Christ our Lord. Amen. (From *Book of Common Prayer,* 1790, Anglican)

## Old Testament Scripture Readings

There I will meet with the people of Israel, and it shall be sanctified by my glory; I will consecrate the tent of meeting and the altar; Aaron also and his sons I will consecrate, to serve me as priests. And I will dwell among the people of Israel, and will be their God. And they shall know that I am the Lord their God, who brought them forth out of the land of Egypt that I might dwell among them; I am the Lord their God. (Ex. 29:43-46)

Elijah took his mantle, and rolled it up, and struck the water, and the water was parted to the one side and to the other, till the two of them could go over on dry ground.

When they had crossed, Elijah said to Elisha, "Ask what I shall do for you, before I am taken from you." And Elisha said, "I pray you, let me inherit a double share of your spirit." And he said, "You have asked a hard thing; yet, if you see me as I am being taken from you, it shall be so for you; but if you do not see me, it shall not be so." And as they still went on and talked, behold, a chariot of fire and horses of fire separated the two of them. And Elijah went up by a whirlwind into heaven. And Elisha saw it and cried, "My father, my father! the chariots of Israel and its horsemen!" And he saw him no more.

Then he took hold of his own clothes and rent
them in two pieces. And he took up the mantle of
Elijah that had fallen from him, and went back and
stood on the bank of the Jordan. Then he took the
mantle of Elijah that had fallen from him, and
struck the water, saying, "Where is the Lord, the
God of Elijah?" And when he had struck the water,
the water was parted to the one side and to the other;
and Elisha went over. (2 Kings 2:8-14)

After the death of Moses the servant of the Lord,
the Lord said to Joshua the son of Nun, Moses'
minister, "Moses my servant is dead; now therefore
arise, go over this Jordan, you and all this people,
into the land which I am giving to them, to the
people of Israel. Every place that the sole of your foot
will tread upon I have given to you, as I promised to
Moses. From the wilderness and this Lebanon as far
as the great river, the river Euphrates, all the land of
the Hittites to the Great Sea toward the going down
of the sun shall be your territory. No man shall be
able to stand before you all the days of your life; as I
was with Moses, so I will be with you; I will not fail
you or forsake you. Be strong and of good courage;
for you shall cause this people to inherit the land
which I swore to their fathers to give them. Only be
strong and very courageous, being careful to do
according to all the law which Moses my servant
commanded you; turn not from it to the right hand
or to the left, that you may have good success
wherever you go. This book of the law shall not
depart out of your mouth, but you shall meditate on
it day and night, that you may be careful to do
according to all that is written in it; for then you

shall make your way prosperous, and then you shall
have good success. Have I not commanded you? Be
strong and of good courage; be not frightened, neither be dismayed; for the Lord your God is with you
wherever you go." (Josh. 1:1-9)

Now the word of the Lord came to me saying,
"Before I formed you in the womb I knew you,
and before you were born I consecrated you;
I appointed you a prophet to the nations."
Then I said, "Ah, Lord God! Behold, I do not know
how to speak, for I am only a youth." But the Lord
said to me,
"Do not say, 'I am only a youth';
for to all to whom I send you you shall go,
and whatever I command you you shall speak,
Be not afraid of them,
for I am with you to deliver you,
        says the Lord."
Then the Lord put forth his hand and touched my
mouth; and the Lord said to me,
"Behold, I have put my words in your mouth.
See, I have set you this day over nations and over
    kingdoms,
to pluck up and to break down,
to destroy and to overthrow,
to build and to plant."
(Jer. 1:4-10)

## New Testament Scripture Readings

Now in the church at Antioch there were prophets
and teachers, Barnabas, Simeon who was called
Niger, Lucius of Cyrene, Manaen a member of the
court of Herod the tetrarch, and Saul. While they
were worshiping the Lord and fasting, the Holy

Spirit said, "Set apart for me Barnabas and Saul for the work to which I have called them." Then after fasting and praying they laid their hands on them and sent them off.

So, being sent out by the Holy Spirit, they went down to Seleucia; and from there they sailed to Cyprus. (Acts 13:1-4)

For we are not, like so many, peddlers of God's word; but as men of sincerity, as commissioned by God, in the sight of God we speak in Christ. (2 Cor. 2:17)

And he called to him his twelve disciples and gave them authority over unclean spirits, to cast them out, and to heal every disease and every infirmity. . . .

"Behold, I send you out as sheep in the midst of wolves; so be wise as serpents and innocent as doves. Beware of men; for they will deliver you up to councils, and flog you in their synagogues, and you will be dragged before governors and kings for my sake, to bear testimony before them and the Gentiles. When they deliver you up, do not be anxious how you are to speak or what you are to say; for what you are to say will be given to you in that hour; for it is not you who speak, but the Spirit of your Father speaking through you. (Matt. 10:1,16-20)

Hence I remind you to rekindle the gift of God that is within you through the laying on of my hands; for God did not give us a spirit of timidity but a spirit of power and love and self-control.

Do not be ashamed then of testifying to our Lord, nor of me his prisoner, but share in suffering for the gospel in the power of God, who saved us and called us with a holy calling, not in virtue of our works but in virtue of his own purpose and the grace which he gave us in Christ Jesus ages ago, and now has manifested through the appearing of our Savior Christ Jesus, who abolished death and brought life and immortality to light through the gospel. For this gospel I was appointed a preacher and apostle and teacher, and therefore I suffer as I do. But I am not ashamed, for I know whom I have believed, and I am sure that he is able to guard until that Day what has been entrusted to me. (2 Tim. 1:6-12)

## Authorizations for Ordination

After due examination and prayer, we confirm the call of this person (or these persons) into the office of pastor/deacon(s) and charge that he (they) be supported by this church in accordance with New Testament practice.

The following brethren (or sisters, or the singular may be used here and throughout) have been duly approved by _____ (here shall be named the authority for the ordination, with the day and place of meeting) as those to whom the Ministry of the Gospel should be committed. By direction of the Church, therefore, I present these brethren for Ordination to the Holy Ministry. (From *Occasional Services*, 1982, Lutheran)

_____ has presented himself to an Ordination Examining Council that was duly called and properly constituted. The Examining Council heard the candidate's statement of Christian experience, call to ministry, views of Christian doctrine and his relationship to our denomination. After due ex-

amination and prayer, the council has affirmed his
call of God to fulfil the duties of a minister in
accordance with New Testament practice. (From *A
Manual for Worship and Service,* 1976, Canadian
Baptist)

## Doxologies

"Hallelujah! Salvation and glory and power belong
    to our God,
for his judgments are true and just." (Rev. 19:1-2)


Now to him who by the power at work within us is
able to do far more abundantly than all that we ask
or think, to him be glory in the church and in Christ
Jesus to all generations, for ever and ever. Amen.
(Eph. 3:20-21)


He remembered for their sake his covenant,
    and relented according to the abundance of his
        steadfast love.
He caused them to be pitied
    by all those who held them captive.


Save us, O Lord our God,
    and gather us from among the nations,
that we may give thanks to thy holy name
    and glory in thy praise.


Blessed be the Lord, the God of Israel,
    from everlasting to everlasting!
And let all the people say, "Amen!"
    Praise the Lord!
(Ps. 106:45-48)

*A hymn of praise may be said or sung, for example:*

Praise the Lord! ye heav'ns, adore him;
Praise him, angels, in the height;
Sun and moon, rejoice before him;
Praise him, all ye stars of light.
Praise the Lord! for he hath spoken;
Worlds his mighty voice obeyed;
Law which never shall be broken
For their guidance hath he made.

Praise the Lord! for he is glorious;
Never shall his promise fail;
God hath made his saints victorious;
Sin and death shall not prevail.
Praise the God of our salvation!
Hosts on high, his power proclaim;
Heav'n and earth and all creation
Laud and magnify his name.
(Words anonymous, adapted from Psalm 148)

## Laying on of Hands

*The symbolic value of this act is that the gospel messengers of one generation pass on God's blessing and power to those who will follow after them. Though words are by no means required, a brief charge, blessing, or covenant would be appropriate:*

May you have God's wisdom and power as you serve him. May your every act be in his will. May your life be enriched by your ministry to others.

May you receive God's richest blessings throughout your Christian ministry.

Since you are now becoming an ordained servant
of God, set apart for work in the Kingdom of God, I
promise to pray for you not only in the immediate
future but throughout your entire ministry.

## Benedictions

*The ordained may offer the closing prayer as a
benediction:*

To the only God, our Savior through Jesus Christ,
our Lord, be glory, majesty, dominion, and authority,
before all time and now and for ever. Amen. (Jude
25)

Blessed be the God and Father of our Lord Jesus
Christ, who has blessed us in Christ with every
spiritual blessing in the heavenly places, even as he
chose us in him before the foundation of the world,
that we should be holy and blameless before him.
(Eph. 1:3-4)

I have been crucified with Christ; it is no longer I
who live, but Christ who lives in me; and the life I
now live in the flesh I live by faith in the Son of God,
who loved me and gave himself for me. (Gal. 2:20)

**Note**

1. By *pastors* and *pastoral ministries*, I refer to most full-time
church staff members, leaving the word *ministers* to apply to all
Christians.

MARION D. ALDRIDGE, a native of Savannah, Georgia, is pastor of First Baptist Church, Batesburg, South Carolina. He is a member of the Executive Committee, the South Carolina Baptist Convention. Aldridge is active in Lions International in Batesburg and was the recipient of the Batesburg-Leesville Chamber of Commerce Service Award. He is a graduate of Clemson University (B.A.) and The Southern Baptist Theological Seminary (M.Div., D.Min.). Aldridge and his wife, Sarah Craig, have two children: Jenna Elizabeth and Julie Rebecca.